Transnational Muslims in American Society

Aminah Beverly McCloud

University Press of Florida
Gainesville/Tallahassee/Tampa/Boca Raton
Pensacola/Orlando/Miami/Jacksonville/Ft. Myers

[redacted]

11 10 09 08 07 06 6 5 4 3 2 1

A record of cataloging-in-publication data is available from the Library of Congress.

ISBN 0-8130-2971-6

The University Press of Florida is the scholarly publishing agency for the State University System of Florida, comprising Florida A&M University, Florida Atlantic University, Florida Gulf Coast University, Florida International University, Florida State University, University of Central Florida, University of Florida, University of North Florida, University of South Florida, and University of West Florida.

University Press of Florida
15 Northwest 15th Street
Gainesville, FL 32611-2079
http://www.upf.com

[redacted]

Dedication

This book is dedicated to those communities, especially Muslims, for whom the horror of genocide is an enduring reality. Special note is made here of the plight of the Muslims of Champa, who are now called Cambodian Muslims when they are spoken of at all.

Champa Muslims are all but erased from history, indeed erased from all world and regional maps. Knowledge of their existence as a Muslim community has been systematically erased by a process of successful total cultural annihilation similar to that attempted by Serbs on Bosnia. The few salvaged artifacts of their culture are in the French National Archives and the Library of the Ecole Française d'Extreme Orient. Champa was a kingdom situated in the center of what is now Vietnam that reached the zenith of its civilization between the sixth and eleventh centuries C.E. Serial losses of land to invaders destroyed the physical presence of their civilization and dispersed all who were not murdered or enslaved. Since the 1960s, Champa Muslims have been forced either to leave Cambodia or to be killed, at first by the Khmer Rouge and then by the Cambodian government. About three thousand Champa Muslims have found refuge in the United States. This book is dedicated to them.

Contents

1

Introduction to Immigrant American Muslims

The study of history is a powerful antidote to contemporary arrogance. It is humbling to discover how many of our glib assumptions, which seem to us novel and plausible, have been tested before, not once but many times and in innumerable guises; and discovered to be, wholly false.[1]

In every undergraduate class I have taught on Islam for the past fourteen years, over four thousand students, the majority (75–80 percent) initially come with little general knowledge of the religion of Islam or the civilization it spawned, other than what they may have gleaned from the few documentaries on television, and even less knowledge about the beliefs and practices of Muslims. It is even difficult for non-Muslim students to reconcile what they hear and read about Muslims and Islam with the behaviors of their Muslim classmates. While my experience in teaching Islamic studies to undergraduates in the largest Catholic university in the United States may be unique in many ways, I suspect that my experiences are the norm.

Among the evident problems in teaching about historical Islam and Muslims in their various cultures remains the paucity of audio-visual materials and texts suitable for introductory university study.[2] Many of the current introductory texts on Islam present a worldview from regional perspectives with bias and with errors. Cultural studies on Islam in America or Islam anywhere outside of a few Arab states are sparse and mostly unavailable outside university bookstores. In large bookstore chains, the section on Islam is always pitifully small even after September 11, 2001. What has grown is the section on terrorism and Muslims, anti-Islam texts, and polemical texts on Muslim cultures.

The fact that Islam and Muslims in the United States is a four-hundred-year-old story is a well-kept historical secret. Only three texts to date tell the story of African Muslim slaves in the United States and these texts are only found outside university bookstores.[3] Cultural inquiries of the life experiences, religious and political, of Muslims in the United States are still too few in number. The tragic events of September 11, 2001, have encouraged more critiques of Islam, analysis of violence in Muslim countries, domestic and foreign policy analyses regarding Muslims, and a spate of fiction demonizing Islam and Muslims.[4] Muslims are currently labeled as either "good" or "bad," radical or extremist (sometimes both), moderate, fundamentalist or militant, and sometimes all of the above.

After September 11, 2001, no less a person than President of the United States George W. Bush engaged in the labeling of Muslims. His "us" versus "them," "good" versus "evil" rhetoric pits the *good* Christian West against an *evil* Islam all over the world. The discourse that has come to surround Islam and Muslims is Orwellian and Machiavellian.[5] But we must remember that the building of blatant intolerance for Islam and Muslims in the United States began in earnest at least a decade ago during the first Bush presidency in the preparations for the Gulf War. In propaganda for this war many lies and half-truths were told to obtain a foothold in the most sacred of Muslim lands, Arabia.[6] On the other hand, the Muslim world is in turmoil and chaos as it engages in its own period of reform and renewal. Most telling are the rise of internal terrorism, the continuing dilemmas of poverty and illiteracy, and the call to go back to the days of Prophet Muhammad as the most excellent of communities. This current reform/renewal era with all of its strife has spilled out onto the West. The West is still involved in suppressing the desires of the masses of those people through its support of corrupt leaderships in its quest to dominant the world's oil resources, many of which are in the Muslim world.

Muslims in the United States have been categorized according to religious adherence, political ideology, class, ethnicity, and place of birth; yet there remains great difficulty in asserting how many Muslims live in the United States. According to a very recent demographic report, "there are 5,745,100 Muslim men and women of all ages living in the United States. Of these, only 3,953,651, or about 69 percent, were born citizens."[7] This population is unevenly distributed across the United States with the majority living in only eleven states. One study claims that the largest single ethnic group is of Arab origin at 32 percent, while other researchers assert that African Americans comprise the largest group at 42 percent.[8] Regardless of the accuracy or inaccuracy of these estimates, Muslims in the United States represent over eighty countries, including the United States, and are representative of almost every conceivable aspect of Muslim thought, from the very conservative reliance on one set of interpretations to the very liberal explorations of many interpretations. They are religious and nonreligious, Republican, Democrat, Independent, and apolitical in varying combinations about domestic and foreign affairs. Practicing Muslims are liberal about some issues and conservative about other issues. There is no "one size fits all," for Muslims in the United States. This text explores the story of Muslims who have migrated to the United States, their children who were born there, and America as host country to Muslim immigrants.

Various ethnic immigrant groups and their religious, political, and economic understandings and yearnings have always shaped much of what is considered American culture, for better or worse. Yet, "up until 1870, American citizenship was granted exclusively to white male persons."[9] These white males and their families came from largely Protestant western European countries seeking religious and political freedom along with economic opportunity. There is little doubt that writers of the U.S. Constitution such as Thomas Jefferson, James Madison, Benjamin Franklin, and John Hancock included clear articulations of their personal religious and nonreligious visions as foundations for U.S. society that rose in stark contrast to Europe but were conceived of as the province of white landowning males. The goal in the new land was to turn opportunity into fortune while escaping religious persecution. While most immigrants brought simple notions about personal and religious freedoms, they also brought notions of family that included the establishment of social, political, and economic institutions to make them viable in an ethnically and religiously competitive environment. These efforts resulted in family-owned businesses such as Sears & Roebuck as well as in crime organizations such as the Gambino family. None in the initial groups of immigrants were considered "alien," that is, nonhuman, though each group had to prove itself worthy of the potential opportunities America offered.

Lisa Lowe, in her study of Asian immigrants, asserts that the word *alien* is a "metonym" for those "who by definition cannot be imagined as sharing in America."[10] America is a diaspora shaped by an imagination of a racially homogeneous society of immigrants despite the presence of Native Americans and an African slave labor force and in the face of their own diverse ethnic and religious backgrounds. We can see that that imagination shifted from a focus on religious freedom to a need for racial exclusivity in law. As "whiteness" became a category for citizenship and thus for entry, Arabs and Asians found themselves vying for the claim. I will discuss in more detail later how "belonging" is synonymous with "whiteness." Though Arabs were first "Asiatic" for twenty years, they became white (until recently). Conversely, South Asians were first categorized as white, then Asian. Nevertheless, both groups' immigration was restricted equally by the National Origins Act of 1924 for four decades until 1965. Racial categories, on almost every local or national document, set the tone for life in the United States and profoundly influenced the shape of the experiences of many immigrants.

The class of immigrants at one level of discourse involves types, including: opportunity seekers, guest workers, refugees, exiles, and illegals. At another level the discussion focuses on the movements of peoples around the world, their remissions of money back to the "homelands," and the subsequent changes in the "back home" family's financial status, along with the issues of life as a transnational. In this exploration of immigrant American Muslims, I have found the term *immigrant* problematic on a number of levels. My major concern is that the term *immigrant* implies a product of movement that is not quite accurate enough for inclusion of the transnational networks formed by most families and discussed for over a decade in anthropology and economics. Though they emigrate to countries across the world, their allegiances are to family and country of origin, rather than to this country as has been our past experiences with immigrants here in the United States. The new immigrants' focus is on the events and experiences of the family network. Some of the subcategories of immigration are also confusing.

For instance, even though the term *immigrant* includes refugees, there is little distinction made between the driving forces of refugees and their resources versus those of economic opportunists. In the United States we comprehend immigrant as a transitional stage in acculturation and have tended to mark degrees of that transition as such in the degree of English language acquisition. We also expect that immigrants, cutting ties with their countries of origin, are making the United States a permanent home. We have continued to use the term *immigrant* with little qualification, and I think that perhaps we, in religious studies, should consider using the subcategories more regularly along with some terms in migration and diaspora studies, such as *transnational*, which are more accurate.

Accurately describing the lives, successful and unsuccessful, of new citizens and their children should assist us in better figuring out the vagaries of their varying relationships with the host society. There are several definitions of *transnational*, but I chose the following:

> Transnationalism—the formation of social, political, and economic relationships among migrants that span several societies.[11]

Clearly, these relationships or networks are beyond what we usually think of when we use the term *immigrant*, even though the "vocabulary of transnationalism" is almost the same as that of immigration. Here too, we must include the notion of diaspora to give definition to a series of prominent community features. The hallmarks of diaspora according to William Safran include:

> retention of collective memory of the homeland; partial alienation from the host society; aspiration to return to an ancestral homeland; commitment to the maintenance or restoration of that homeland; and derivation of collective consciousness and solidarity from a relationship with the homeland.[12]

Remember, to be eligible for inclusion as a diaspora, the people have to be dispersed from a homeland to two or more other territories and there must be some kind of exchange—social, cultural, or political between the spatially separated populations from the same homeland.

It is important, however, to reassert that it is the quality and quantity of networks that determine the quality of life in the diaspora. For example, most African immigrants remit significant portions of their income to their families "back home." Yet, their participation in a profitable transnational network is minimal at best, so that the financial transaction is most often a one-way deal. On the other hand, many South Asian Muslims are links in older, significantly more profitable networks in global markets such as real estate, trading, finance, and diamond-selling. They too, send significant amounts of money home, but because of their networks, they are not bankrupted in the process as goods and access to services are sent to them. While the family obligations and the spread of extended family members are the same, the resources of support are significantly different.

So, immigrant Muslims are better described as diasporan Muslims who are transnationals, some of whom are refugees, and exiles. While they are committed to the "maintenance and restoration" of their homelands, they also develop varying degrees of allegiances to their host country. A few transnationals and their children follow the paths of assimilation/acculturation while many others do not. Much of this is because the family networks are essential as they provide a sense of belonging, financial resources, and marriage stock. Most are at home in several countries where their parents or siblings live. Few know much of the cultural history of any country outside of the "home" country.

No matter the reason for immigration, the process of learning to live and thrive in foreign (alien) soil is extremely difficult. For Muslim transnationals, everything from brands of cleaning aids to the absence of bargaining is different. The political realm of society is as masked as the social cues of belonging. Imagine, many immigrants, regardless of ethnicity or religious tradition or even network resources, have to negotiate language and its nuances, a different way of living everyday, a different relationship to a new political and economic system, and the absence of the familiar sights, smells, and sounds. This process is exhilarating, tiring, and frightening.

How does an immigrant come to begin to understand the workings of neighborhoods, districts, and the federal government? From my many conversations with transnational Muslims, two notions emerged as priorities: citizenship and success in a profession. It is apparent that the concerns are still personal, which is reflective of the age of this diaspora.[13] The events of September 11, 2001, however, have done little to change the priorities. Some might say that the priorities rather than abating have taken on a heightened meaning. There are skills yet to be learned about competing in the public spaces of a multicultural, multireligious, multiethnic democratic society. In referring to their initial movements in the diaspora, Thomas Sowell asserts:

> To one degree or another, however, immigrants have also tended to assimilate, first with compatriots from different parts of their country of origin, and later with members of the larger society around them in the country where they settled.[14]

I would add that the extreme diversity of the United States has made Sowell's assertion more difficult, and regarding Muslims, the cultural antipathy has made assimilation almost impossible for the near future. Added to the culture shock of immigrating, no matter how familiar the new territory, is the internal cultural shock of the diversity of the Muslim community. The use of those ethnic networks plays a significant role in how they keep old hostilities at bay. After all, most of them come from largely ethnically homogeneous countries that have well-established, state-authorized religious leadership. For many Muslim immigrants, the diversity of Muslims also presents potentially new configurations of power and class not found in many Muslim cultures.

Inquiries of U.S. society as host to Muslim immigrants required me to enlist the knowledge of many of my colleagues across disciplines. I found that by exploring some of the scholarship in the disciplines of anthropology, sociology, and theology, I could summarize the authoritative or at least classical examinations of Muslims that have most informed American thinking. I reviewed movies and film studies to explore the visual imagery that gave Americans pictures of Islam and Muslims. What I found was both disconcerting and, in many instances, apparently helped to provoke some of the present violence toward Muslims. Readers must decide for themselves if scholarship and film's negative depictions are indeed stereotypes of a nature that prevents inclusion of Muslims in the American fabric. Media representation of Muslims, beginning in earnest after 1979, seems to capitalize on the products of scholarship and film depictions, though it has been most damning since September 11, 2001. No other world religion has ever been attacked and rendered evil in the history of America. Even the Christianity of Nazi Germany is not demonized but considered an aberration. The reinvention, distortion, and confusion of language has served to thoroughly confound most non-Muslim Americans about Islam and Muslims.

With all of this in mind, I set out to put in print a summary of what I teach about some of America's Muslim diasporans, along with more recent research. Though I have had many, many conversations over thirty-five years, I started more-focused dialogues with members of various communities about what mattered most to them about their lives as immigrants. Several concerns topped the list. Members of all communities felt that very little of their modern histories are known in the United States and that many non-Muslim Americans could not see them as humans due to the stereotypes and misinformation. To these concerns I added questions of religious understanding and the rationales for choosing the United States for their diaspora.

Given that American Muslims represent over eighty countries, I had to choose whose stories to tell. In my class, "Islam in Global Contexts," students and I get a rare and wonderful opportunity to research Muslims in both predominately Muslim countries and in countries where they are a minority. This course explores the effects on Muslim cultures of communism along with monarchies and military dictatorships. Using the same reasoning, I decided to explore American Muslim cultures in the same way. Thus, we can examine the modern histories of Arabic speakers, South Asian, Chinese, Iranian, and Somali Muslims, and their presence in America. By using this approach I can give at least a hint of the cultural diversity of immigrant Muslims in America. The differences in cultures are dramatic and permit readers some insight to the differences in behavior of diasporan Muslims.

The Arabic-speaking Muslim community is actually composed of a number of smaller national communities that are distinguished by their colonial and modern histories along with their Islamic claims to authority/legitimacy in the Arab world. For example, Egyptians project a portion of their claims to Islamic authority based on the presence of Al-Azhar University in Cairo and its ideological leadership in the Muslim world. South Asians are distinguished more by their modern history and also by the variety of Islamic understandings. South Asians are Sunni, Shiʿite, and Sufi (as are Arabs), and some of them also belong to theologically different Islamic groups that have been declared heretical in the Muslim world but are very influential in the United States such as the Ismaʿilis or Ahmadi. Claims of religious authority and legitimacy are serious issues. Intimate knowledge of the Qur'an, its recitation, and some mastery of the Arabic language have been the hallmark of legitimacy in Islam almost since its inception. Many South Asians learn to read Arabic but without comprehension, and thus falter in one test of legitimacy in the Muslim world. One result is that South Asians, along with numbers of others, are not considered Islamic authorities outside of their homelands or other long-standing diasporas such as that of South Africa. The United States however, is one place of contention of this status as South Asians can claim authority over religious matters, something they can not claim in the Muslim world.

One community that is sizable though not nearly as large as either the Arab or South Asian groups is the Iranian community. A brief examination of this community gives a glimpse of life as exile. During the last shah's reign, an elite, secular class of Muslims was nurtured in Iran. The overthrow of the shah and his government added exiles, self-declared and involuntary, to the U.S. Muslim diaspora. Perhaps they have remained under the radar of many researching Muslim communities because they generally keep to themselves or assimilate almost completely into American society. Those few that keep their Shi'ite Muslim practices have also been the most outspoken on the treatment of Muslims, while many of those who do not practice Islam are equally outspoken against Iran and its theocracy. Irrespective of their personal religious position, the Iranian revolution put Iranians, in the regions where they live in the United States, on the media map.

Selecting smaller research communities was very difficult since there were so many possibilities. I chose Chinese and Somali American Muslims. In the end, this selection is to explore, albeit briefly, Muslims on the margins. Chinese Muslims are a minority in China and a minority even among the Muslims in the United States. Chinese immigrant Muslims come to the United States after having lived as a minority in one of the last Communist states in the world. They survived and multiplied under communist rule in a largely Buddhist land before coming to America. Islam in China developed with both Buddhist and Confucian overtones just as Islam in South Asia bears the obvious imprint of Hinduism.

Somali Muslims were chosen because, though geographically close to the Arab world and largely ethnically homogeneous, they are not considered a part of the authoritative center of Islam. There are only several hundred Christians in predominately Muslim Somalia. Somalis came to the United States mostly as refugees who settled together in places as far apart as Seattle, Washington; Minneapolis, Minnesota; and Lewiston, Maine. They, like other diasporans, set up networks across America. Though they are a relatively old Muslim community, they are not Arabic speakers and look much like the indigenous African-American population. Obviously, their American experience is shaped by their refugee status and the color of their skin. Exploring the contours of each of these communities demands a look at how they interact with each other, with the indigenous communities, and with the larger non-Muslim society. The diversity of world experiences under differing kinds of governments, colonialisms, civil wars, economic strife, and so on has prevented most Muslims from really knowing one another. In the United States, Muslims from over eighty countries try to at least worship together one day a week. While this has not fostered deep mutual understandings, it has opened doors that were closed a few decades ago. With the opening of doors, however, come the inevitable tensions of misunderstandings and competitions. Arabic speakers whose countries have been in dispute with Israel have one set of issues while, for example, Chinese

Muslims are more concerned with United States–China relations. All of the transnational communities however, are concerned with the definition of Islam in America and their place in that definition.

In the United States, where representatives of majority and minority Muslim communities reside as various kinds of immigrants, the notion of *ummah* (world community of Muslims) is under review. Whereas in matters of practice, Muslims can be seen praying together, they listen to the authority of, take console in, and act only for their ethnic community. In the small world of Muslim politics in America, Arabs and South Asians are battling for prominence with little if any consultation with leaders of other communities. Many in both communities voted for George W. Bush in 2000 because of his stance on "family values" and tax relief for the wealthy. Many of the same Muslims did vote for him again for the same reasons despite the unhealthy climate for Muslims in America since his first election. Other Muslim communities have been either staunchly Democrat or Independent or apolitical.

As previously asserted, almost all immigrant Muslims support families in their homeland. Many of these Muslims also support political parties in the homeland along with charitable organizations. The agendas of these political parties vary as do the recipients of the charity. Since September 11, 2001, the support for political parties and charitable organizations has come under intense scrutiny. Some of the findings have not only been eye-opening for non-Muslim Americans, they have been shocking to American Muslims in general. Some Muslims have knowingly supported political groups whose aims are to overthrow existing Muslim governments while others have inadvertently supported the same groups by giving to charitable causes. In general, immigrant American Muslims have been as challenged by their cultural traditions as by their lack of participation in American society. There is an ever expanding chasm between transnational and indigenous Muslims on issues of foreign and domestic policy as well as the definition of Islam. Though this text is not an expose, it will explore some of the questionable activities and positions in the Muslim communities under examination. These activities include issues surrounding public financial malfeasance, race, class, gender, support for terrorism, and so on.

I interviewed members of these communities for their comments on their history, culture, and contemporary issues. These interviews were informal and participation was active. On several occasions I had to return to individuals for clarifications, and on many occasions, individuals contacted me over the two years of research to add to their previous comments. One persistent concern in all of these communities was the definition of Islam in the United States. Many wanted Islam defined as a "peaceful" religion with its values becoming a part of American values. Others wanted Islam defined as "the true religion," placing it in an adversarial position. Still others felt that Islam would further define itself as it emerged as an American religion. Some young Muslims felt that their parents were trying to make Islam "just like it was in their homeland." These responses, interestingly, were not distinguishable by ethnic group or by age or by degree of public religiosity.

Given that the task could yield a small history of the world, I divided the work in several ways. For the sections on Arabic speakers and South Asians, there is a section on modern history followed by a section on life in America. Smaller communities have their modern histories incorporated into their chapters. Each chapter has a subsection on the community's social and professional organizations where present. The last chapter is devoted to a survey of the Muslim diasporic community in the United States and their interactions with each other, with indigenous Muslims, and with the larger non-Muslim society. This chapter examines the concerns of immigrant communities since September 11, 2001, and their hopes for a future in the United States. It is my hope that readers gain a more accurate knowledge of transnational American Muslims.

2

A Nation of Immigrants, Stereotypes, Imaginations

My exploration into America as host society to a number of diasporas and transnationals includes examinations of scholarship and various media as fundamental contributors to American knowledge of Islam and Muslims. Here we have to begin with our treatment of immigrants in general.

> . . . many have perceived that the numbers of immigrants is overwhelming. These perceptions have been repeated by many if not most writers of history texts, who have persisted in using what I call hydraulic metaphors to describe the immigration process. Immigration is almost habitually described as a "flood," or an "inundation," and immigrants are described as coming in "waves," "torrents," and "streams." It is not necessary to be an expert in semantics to understand that one result of the habitual use of such language is to stigmatize immigrants as the "other," rather than as the ancestors of us all.[1]

Immigrants coming in these waves, torrents, and floods are portrayed as drowning, washing out, or overpowering American citizens, and thus, representing a threat to the American way of life. Any story of immigrants must be at minimum a two-culture study of the attitude of the host culture to a particular immigrant group and of the culture of the immigrants. We also now have to consider that some immigrants may also be transnational and that their relationships with the host culture are different from those of other immigrants. The United States is one of an elite group of nations in which others want to live. It is also one of an elite group of nations acting as host to significant diasporas.

> Not like the brazen giant of Greek fame,
> With conquering limbs astride from land to land:
> Here at our sea-washed, sunset gates shall stand
> A mighty woman with a torch, whose flame
> Is the imprisoned lightening, and her name
> Mother of Exiles. From her beacon-hand
> Glows world-wide welcome; her mild eyes command

The air-bridged harbor that twin cities frame.
"Keep, ancient lands, your storied pomp!" cries she
With silent lips. "Give me your tired, your poor,
Your huddled masses yearning to breathe free,
The wretched refuse of your teeming shore.
Send these, the homeless, tempest-tost, to me,
I lift up my lamp beside the golden door!"

Emma Lazarus (d. 1887)

This invitation is, as we know, the result of a history of immigrants. Tired, poor, and huddled men, women, and children, initially from northern and western Europe, have sought refuge (spiritual, political, social, and economic) in the possibilities of this country. Emma Lazarus's poem, engraved on the base of the Statue of Liberty, is both a testament to the view that our society has of itself and the view that it wishes to project to the world, even though it is perhaps a quite utopian one. As a shelter from the storms of European religious intolerance, general social injustice, famines, and general discontent, the United States was and remains a paradise for many immigrants. European and largely Protestant immigrants could keep or shed their former histories and experience "a world of possibilities." Any future that could be imagined was possible.[2] One result of this "world of possibilities" was the elevation of individual effort as the cornerstone of society. It is individual wealth and success that are important, not family wealth or class. The phrase "only in America," sometimes used negatively, really reflects an unheard of freedom—the space to re-create oneself without family, or ties to any "thing." The American dream has been and is a reality for many, even recent, immigrants. Individuals are also expected to understand and act on the facts that sometimes families, particular religious adherences, class status, and so on, are usually obstacles that have to be confronted and in many cases overcome in order to succeed. Immigrants are further expected to shed those values of their former lives that do not comport with American values, however vaguely defined. In this American "possibility of being," the autonomous individual is extolled in national narratives and in classic films as an American norm.[3]

Yet this nation's invited immigrants, many of whom are transnationals, have not had an easy time.[4] Cross-cultural interaction, even between immigrants from Europe, has presented difficulties most manifest in the development of a rather paradoxical, racialized, public culture—at once cherishing of and ambivalent about difference. Though Ms. Lazarus herself may have created her words to encompass more than northern Europe, U.S. public culture and immigration law has been quite unambiguous about who is acceptable for sharing in the "possibilities" and who is unacceptable. Not all immigrants are welcome, no matter how tired, poor, talented, or wretched. There has always been an internal aversion to "people of color" as proved by chattel slavery, genocide against Native Americans, Jim Crow, the creation of reservations and ghettos for containment, and the introduction of race into immigration law. This aversion was extended to the world. Yet the statue remains in the harbor with its invitation.[5]

> The Immigration Act of 1882 was the first general law upon the subject, provided for the exclusion from the United States of the following classes only: Convicts, lunatics, idiots, and persons likely to become a public charge.[6]

The need for additions to the above exclusions came with more immigrants from southern Europe. In subsequent immigration laws, many new classes for exclusion appear, as does the curious term *alien*. Along with categories of mental defect (imbecile and the feebleminded) and the sick (those with tuberculosis and epilepsy) is added "persons who practice, believe in or advocate the practice of polygamy." Finally, race is added as a category overriding the rest of the excludable classes.

> There developed as time went on an even greater concern as to the fundamental racial character of the constantly increasing numbers who came. The record of alien arrivals year by year had shown a gradual falling off in the immigration of northwest European peoples, representing racial stocks that were common to America even in colonial days and a rapid and remarkably large increase in the movement from southern and eastern European countries and Asiatic Turkey.[7]

In Section 2169 of the Revised Statutes under Title XXX of the Naturalization Act, the issues of "free white persons" in addition to African-descended persons as eligible for naturalization are given definition.[8] The racial preference stands alongside the celebrations of shared experiences such as conquering the land, the war of independence, religious and political debates, and the triumph of the individual over adversity as aspects of national identity. Our national identity has stood in various historical times to protect us from a number of others including Communists, the Japanese, and now the Muslims. Even the 1924 National Origins Quota system was designed to favor immigrants from northern Europe while restricting those from southern Europe and "colored" countries. It was not until 1965, as one of the products of the Civil Rights/Black Power era, that this system was repealed and family reunification put forth as the core of immigration policy.

Also during this time, two strategies came together to produce opportunities for tens of thousands of Muslims to emigrate to the United States. As some Muslims, especially South Asians and Arabs, were able to take advantage of family reunification policies, many others were able to emigrate because we needed their skills especially in medicine, computer science, and engineering. This infusion of skill and subsequent wealth has shaped the immigrant Muslim community as one of the wealthiest and most educated groups of immigrants.[9] Previously, the issues surrounded race and entry categories. These categories reflect old features of immigration.[10] The old categories provided a context for those left behind. The new categories mentioned in chapter 1 more accurately reflect the global migration of peoples and thus, the newer categories of "withholding," "exile," and so on. The older categories also reflect a stated desire of the immigrant to stay in the United States and become a fully participatory citizen. Globalism has not only spread technology and opportunity, it has spawned a new citizen of the world who sometimes has and sometimes does not have allegiances to a particular place of residence. Yet the expectations from the hosts of these transnationals are the same as those of the immigrant.

Citizenship demands allegiance and guarantees rights to the inhabitants. Noncitizen residents often feel challenged or are challenged by the demands of allegiance while struggling with the absence of guaranteed rights. Partial knowledge of the demands of allegiance and rights often results in a modified freedom, though certainly more than exists in many of their "homelands." The categories in place for those seeking citizenship convey some of the ambiguity toward immigration. Citizens are born or naturalized. Noncitizens are peculiarly designated *aliens*, and then subcategorized as documented into classes—family reunification, refugees (those given visas for entry and asylees—those who came illegally), temporary (documented) aliens—visitors, temporary workers, students, and tourists, and undocumented aliens (illegal aliens). It is worrisome to contemplate the presumptions that attend this naming of humans. Yet the United States is host to a variety of aliens and home to a variety of citizens. One perennial question about immigrants involves whether or not they really understand citizenship.

I must admit that this question was difficult for even me, a citizen, to answer. Citizens learn the definition of citizenship early in school, almost so early that the definition is lost by adulthood. For those of us reaching early adulthood in the 1970s we also learned that, in addition to the differences in citizens based on color, there were also categories of class and gender. Thinking about citizenship, I decided to think (nonscientifically) about people's relationship to government policies. There are citizens who, though certain of their allegiance to the country, can name only a few rights such as voting, Miranda rights, the right to litigate, the right to worship. Obviously there are citizens who are very vocal on rights, domestic and foreign policies, and allegiance to the country. We read about them in magazines and see them on television. Pinpointing the concerns of this second group even further, I found that there is one subgroup that becomes vocal whenever an issue affects race, class, or gender but not often on any combination of the categories; it is always just one marker. For example, some African Americans will protest over an issue that discriminates against them because of their race but those same African Americans will not join in protest over issues that discriminate against women. Similarly, some American women will protest on either side of the abortion issue or discrimination against women but will not take to the streets over worker's rights. These cases typify single-issue citizens.

Thus far I can speculate that the ordinary American's experience of democracy is either the individual experience of voting, military enlistment, or a group experience of protest or support for a cause linked to their group, however defined. But, within the group experience of protest or support, perhaps because it is organized around special interests, the result is often dependent on class and influence. Community activism and wide political interests sometimes cause the emergence of a vocal group of citizens who mature past the nominal experience of voting, past the group special-interest experience who emerge as power brokers or politicians. I am sure these groups are more accurately described in political science literature, but for the purposes of this text, this brief description is sufficient. What do Muslim immigrants understand about this system when they come from countries whose political systems range from monarchies to political dictatorships to quasi democracies? The answer is very little.

The United States as host to millions of immigrants has variously described itself as a "melting pot" and as a "salad bowl." There is the presumption that if one goes through all the trials to become a citizen, that person will be anxious to belong and to be known as an American. Prior to the middle of the twentieth century, immigrants, mostly European, could look like other older immigrants and their descendants simply by changing their dress and keeping relatively quiet in the public square so that their accents were not exposed. Clothing became one indicator of belonging that could be put into use quickly in the public spaces.

> Clothing was no private affair, subject to fancy or the whim of the moment. What one wore was a public construct, bound up with an enduring moral order. Fashion was [and is] an instrument to help people fit in, not stand out. An immigrant donning a starched collar made himself acceptable . . . [11]

While this schema worked for Christian European immigrants as an entry level of belonging in the public square, later immigrants from other parts of the world have had difficulty sometimes because of color and dress and other times because of religion. Immigrant Muslim women, especially those who wear veils, have become enigmatic symbols of difference. Many veiled immigrant Muslim women brave the stares, vulgar talk, and spitting that comes from other Americans when they are in the public space without the impulse to remove the veil. For some, as the tensions heighten post–September 11, 2001, their determination to remain veiled increases in direct proportion to the hostility toward them in the public space.[12] The otherness of their dress, even though modest by all accounts, is seen as a challenge by some in American society and there is pressure to "hurry up" and become American—change your dress. The pressure on all immigrant communities is to show signs of assimilation especially in language and dress. Lack of obvious assimilation, as in a change of dress, is still regarded as confirmation of their otherness. Rhetoric denigrating Islam and labeling Muslims as terrorists and thus creating a host of stereotypes and imaginations abounds, but the background for what is now stated with impunity began in the early cinema.

Since September 11, 2001, an even more hateful rhetoric has come to describe transnational American Muslims adding to the discourse on Islam and Muslims already created in scholarship and media. Previously called "talkies" and "moving pictures" (at the beginning of the twentieth century), going to the movies included a feature movie and later a series of newsreels that conveyed particular views of domestic and foreign events aimed to forge opinions on issues, while the movies did the same in an entertaining way.

Stereotypes and Imagination

In the early twentieth century, movie depictions, as in *The Birth of a Nation,* documented American chattel slaves as "happy, loyal, and inept" thus, making "freed Negroes" a new challenge to be controlled. *Modern Times,* starring Charlie Chaplin, presented the protest against and struggles with industrialization and modernization. Chaplin clearly saw the power of progress, its advancement working to the commoner's detriment. The movies and later cinema also painted vivid pictures of others to give the elite (not everyone could go to the movies then) a sense of moral and technological superiority.

African and Native American men were caricatured variously as docile servants, sex-crazed maniacs, or violent terrorists. Both groups of men were internal threats to the civilizing of the land and the progress of its (white) people. Whites were (and still are) represented as mostly rugged individuals and adventurers willing to risk their lives to affirm their own freedom from restraint and to pursue opportunity (economic and political). Certainly, there were "bad" white guys who had no conscience—who killed and robbed without remorse. We have made many of them national heroes as "the cowboys"—part of the national drama of conquering the "west" (the frontier). Even some of the "bad" guys were really "good" white guys "gone bad" from the ravages of war, like Jesse James.

In *Visions of the East,* Matthew Bernstein leads readers in a discussion of "western" portrayals of the "east" at the beginning of the twentieth century that is important for our examination of immigrant American Muslims.[13] Bernstein notes that American feelings toward the Orient, while not the product of "a long tradition of . . . Orientalism," as with the British and the French, make up for lost time with equally denigrating portrayals of those cultures.

The "Orient" served Americans as another "other." Despite lack of involvement in European imperialisms, the taste of blood and power were present from the colonial and slave experiences.

> Western narrative and ethnographic cinemas of the late nineteenth and twentieth centuries inherited the narrative and visual traditions, as well as the cultural assumptions, on which Orientalism was based, and filmmakers discovered how popular Orientalism could be.[14]

American cinemas, like their European counterparts, also served "to reinforce the sense of national identity."

During this early-twentieth-century period, the United States was engaged in a series of internal transformations in the process of identity formation made necessary by the Civil War, industrialization, and inventions. By the 1920s electricity had been harnessed to light streets and homes and to run appliances; the toilet was now indoors, new roads were paved, rail lines extended, the telegraph modernized, and the first telephone had been installed in the White House. The legacies of New England Puritanism, during this same period, set the standard in differentiating the American way of working, attitudes toward women, and behavior in the public space. Even women were one critical focus in this attempt to set a different standard as advertisements, literature, and the church exhorted them to take seriously their duty to raise their children and be morally sensible, pure, and socially active rather than become active in the process of modernizing and be exposed to radicalism and the Bolsheviks.

Another factor during this period that contributed to the formation of a unique American identity was scholarship on religion. "From the beginning of national life, religion had served as a bond of unity that helped overcome the divisive effects of competing local interests and regional concerns."[15] Yet in the post–Civil War era, religion competed with evolution and technology as the authority and the authoritative in the society. Consequently, during the first decades of the twentieth century, among religious leaders and intellectuals there was "a sense of a profound spiritual and cultural crisis."[16] According to George Marsden, "just after the Civil War, mainstream evangelical Protestantism was still the dominant religious force in American life." Alternatively and simultaneously, new forms of Protestantism emerged such as the Social Gospel movement and fundamentalism, the former to combat poverty and economic injustice and the latter to return the populace to the Bible in the face of modernization.[17] While both these forms of Christianity reigned for decades above and below the public radar, they were both also handmaidens of modernity.

In an era of rapid technological advancement, increased pluralism, increased possibilities for women, a declining interest in God, and a "drastically altered" intellectual climate, the need for a national identity was critical. This national identity has been concretized in a short time, perhaps too short a time. In this politically pluralistic and multicultural society, one voice, one image became paramount in the public space. Movies, books, and newspapers set much of the public image.

The United States as host community in the first half of the twentieth century used the light in its harbor to welcome immigrants from Europe and begrudgingly admit immigrants from other parts of the world. In her efforts to build a society with a particular racial stock but also one that needed the skills and labor of others, she continually modified immigration laws. As previously stated by Bernstein, scholars of the cinema assert that the United States "inherited the narrative and visual traditions, as well as the cultural assumptions" of Europe regarding the construct of the Orient.[18]

Interestingly, "the Orient" as delineated in film focused on the Arab world (and continues to do so), and currently much of the scholarly literature on Muslims in the world singles out Muslims living in the Arab states around the state of Israel, especially Palestine (the only nonstate), Egypt, Jordan, Iraq, and Syria and the only non-Arab state of Iran. This shrinking of the Muslim world to Arab states is reflected prominently in the cinema. As a result, a large percentage of what I can say about the United States as host to a Muslim diaspora is also framed by what has been identified as the Muslim world—those particular Arab states. This American focus gave birth to the syllogism, all Arabs are threatening and the other; all Arabs are Muslim; thus all Muslims are threatening and the other.

The subcontinent (an inaccurate term to say the least) is treated very differently in American cinema and in the public discourse on Muslims. South Asians, until recently, have been virtually absent as Muslims in cinema or public discourse. Hindus, Muslims, Christians, Jains, Sikhs, and Buddhists are all generally treated in the abstract category of "Hindoos," when they are seen at all in movies. Even today, with all the fears of terrorists and the labeling of Pakistan as a home for Muslim terrorists, this still holds generally true as most Americans cannot distinguish between South Asian religions and have only minimal knowledge of the region. Though many South Asian Muslim women wear veils and are in the background of movies such as the Indiana Jones series, they are still "Hindoos."

Scholarship on "the East," "the Orient," or Muslims is found most predominately in anthropology, regional histories, and theology. Philologists, the ancestors of many anthropologists, asserted developmental categories for the world using their own (Western) cultures as the norm. Nineteenth-century ethnographers used these categories in their studies of world cultures and moral development. According to Alan Nadel in *Visions of the East*,

> the [more] morally "advanced" a nation or race, the higher on the developmental scale, the more capable of founding sophisticated political institutions, and the more fitted for government it would be. And the higher the moral qualities its members would demonstrate.[19]

We know that American scholarly interest in "the East" or "the Orient" significantly increased by World War II. In the United States, the idea of the "Orient" not only presented a contrasting image, it enabled a broad political, economic, and social agenda—*tiers monde* (stratification of the world) into first, second, and third worlds.[20] The United States inherited the mantle of imperialism after World War II and had to establish itself as a world power on its way to being the world's only superpower. Much of the scholarship on the world outside of America ceased to have any hint of objectivity. As the "west" moved to appear more benevolent, scholars worked to soften the vocabulary of imperialism and unfortunately the replacements were equally condescending.

> Substitutions like that of the word "traditional" for "primitive" were part of a general Western tendency to clean up the language of government, journalism, and social science in reference to the rest of the world. Terms evoking ethnocentrism, condescension, imperialism, and aggression were systematically replaced by apparently neutral and scientific terms—euphemisms. "Former colonies" became "developing nations" while "primitive tribes" became "traditional peoples."[21]

The first world is the most democratic and free; a model for the second and third worlds to follow. Most importantly, the first world is relatively unrestrained by the chains of state religion or ideology. A second world—the former

Soviet Union, China, Japan, and tiny Cuba—occupy a peculiar space. They are like us, but not like us because of their adherence to state ideology and its expression through totalitarianism. The third world is the rest of the world regardless of state religion or ideology or presence of democratic institutions, and it has certain characteristics. People in the third world are religious, living largely in poverty (although this could also be said about China) and resistant to the modernity of the West. We Americans quickly forget our own difficulties with modernity and technology.

Once we had the scholarship to affirm our categorizations, European history was positioned as the locus of all other histories. Even American educational curricula affirm this conclusion.

> We know how the traditional story runs; history began in the "East"—in Mesopotamia and Egypt (but not paradise, still further east, as the medieval Westerners had said); the torch was then passed successively to Greece and Rome and finally to the Christians of northwestern Europe, where medieval and modern life developed. During the Middle Ages, Islam temporarily was permitted to hold the torch of science, which properly belonged to the West, until the West was ready to take it over and carry it forward. India, China, and Japan also had ancient civilizations but were isolated from the mainstream of history and "contributed" still less to it (that is to Western Europe). In modern times Western Europe expanded over the rest of the world, so that Islam and India and China have ceased to be isolated, and have entered the orbit of the ongoing Western civilization, now becoming a world civilization.[22]

European historians and cartographers succeeded in making Europe both a continent and the center of the world. Americans made the United States a huge country, and for American students *it* is the center, and only those countries with whom America has had successful contact are worthy of study and then in very limited ways. With "the West" as the locus of industrialization, modernization, and technology, the historical achievements of the rest of the world are again isolated and, worse yet, forgotten. It is where "Western" scholars focus their sight that is important. In "Western" divisions of the world, the East, or rather "the Orient," is categorized as Near, Middle, and Far—from the West. Regarding Islam, the eye settled on the Mediterranean and that section of northern Africa that has been dubbed "the Middle East." The focus on the Mediterranean even managed to divide that culture. Muslims in the region share with Greeks, Italians, Portuguese, and others a culture of family loyalty, honor, and shame, yet Muslims are heralded as being somehow different.

Our imagings do not stop with our divisions of the world. As mentioned earlier, anthropological researches have been one of the primary contributors to our imaginings of the exotic.[23] They created a fantasy space in "the lure of far-distant lands" while casting the dimension of historical time as nonexistent. What we saw in the movies about Islam and Muslims did not happen hundreds of years ago but was occurring in the present and depicted every Muslim anywhere. The "other" lives far away and, thus, has no contact with "civilization," "modernity," or "technology." Sarah Graham-Brown asserts:

> One of the central features of this vision of the Orient, which is most evident in popular writings and visual imagery, but which also informed many works of scholarship, was the concept of a society where all aspects of life—culture, politics, economics and personal relationships—could be explained by reference to the religion of Islam. In this essentialist view, Islam offered an explanatory touchstone for the behavior of people from otherwise diverse cultures, ethnic groups and social classes.[24]

This anthropological view was at its height during the era of European colonialism but continues in its production of accounts of travel, photography, and literature on the region defined as "the Middle East" for the twenty-first century. Other parts of the world where Muslims live are characterized as different others. The "Middle East" has been the central focus for a long time. Travelers like Mark Twain had already labeled the "home" of Arabs as a place of fantasy where the able could have indescribable adventures.

> We wanted something thoroughly and uncompromisingly foreign—foreign from top to bottom—foreign from centre to circumference—foreign inside and outside and all around—nothing anywhere about it to dilute its foreignness—nothing to remind us of any other people or any other land under the sun. And lo! In Tangiers we have found it.[25]

While the "Middle East" has always been portrayed as a violent other, the tragic events of September 11, 2001, added *terroristic* to the list of adjectives, thus making the region a totally undesirable place and Islam an unredeemably violent religion. The use of this kind of language when referring to Islam and Muslims is not new. Also not new are the problems between Christianity and Islam. British scholar of international repute and former nun Karen Armstrong lends her thoughts in tracing evidence of this hostility and asserts:

> In this fear-ridden fantasy, Muhammad was an impostor and a charlatan, who had set himself up as a prophet to deceive the world; he was a lecher

> who had wallowed in disgusting debauchery and inspired his followers to do the same; he had forced people to convert to his faith at sword point.
>
> To explain Muhammad's success, the legends claimed that he had been a magician who had concocted false "miracles" to take in the credulous Arabs and destroy the Church in Africa and the Middle East.[26]

As inheritors of much of this theological discourse, some Christian Americans quite naturally overlook the central claims of Islam. Edward Said, himself an Orthodox Christian Arab and public intellectual pointed out,

> For most of the Middle Ages and during the early part of the Renaissance in Europe, Islam was believed to be a demonic religion of apostasy, blasphemy, and obscurity. It did not seem to matter that Muslims considered Mohammad a prophet and not a god; what mattered to Christians was that Mohammad was a false prophet, a sower of discord, a sensualist, a hypocrite, and an agent of the devil.[27]

Though this is not the Middle Ages, there is ample evidence of concrete and pervasive hostility toward Islam that can clearly be seen in the works of some contemporary scholars. Armstrong points out one of these scholars, Conor Cruise O'Brien, considered by Western scholars as knowledgeable on Islam in Africa. In an article in the *New York Times* (11 May 1989) speaking about Muslim society, he asserts:

> Looks profoundly repulsive. . . . It looks repulsive because it is repulsive. . . . A Westerner who claims to admire Muslim society, while still adhering to Western values, is either a hypocrite or an ignoramus or a bit of both.[28]

This statement of repulsion, apparently assisted by media, is equally true in the events in Columbus, Ohio, during the week of July 19, 2004. Outside the City Hall, a group of socially conservative Christians from around the nation gathered to "protest abortion, gay rights and the Islamic faith." They burned a Qur'an along with a gay-pride flag and a copy of the Roe *v.* Wade decision to show their angst. President Bush's "crusades-talk" has worked well with the media, which serves him without much question in the effort to depict Islam and Muslims as violent and other.

Since the latter half of the twentieth century, media—cinema, print, and broadcast—have become the preferred vehicles of knowledge about the world. Regarding Muslims, the syllogism has been endlessly perpetuated, with violence as the only action of an entire world civilization other than abuse of its women.

David Hume (political philosopher, 1711–1776) emphasized the problems with and concerns about reasoning in this way.

> Hume emphasized that the expectation of one thing following another does not lie in the things themselves, but in our mind. And expectation . . . is associated with habit.[29]

Jostein Gaarder uses a simple example to explain Hume on this point. Hume is speaking about "natural law"—the laws of nature—cause and effect that is necessary for our understanding of these issues.

> Well, because I have seen a whole herd of black horses doesn't mean that all horses are black.[30]

Regarding Islam and/or Muslims, the media has used natural law to explain an enormously diverse group of people who live all over the world as all the same. All Muslims are Arab, ruled by a violent religion: Islam, which endorses oppression of women, hatred for the West, and indiscriminate violence against the innocent.

The role media play as primary disseminators of the facts is critical to our current enterprise of empire building. Various mass media, but especially television, are our principal teachers as they serve many purposes—individual opinions (the producers) are taken and "forged into communal sentiments;" they "teach us what is 'real' and what we value." How do media accomplish all these things so essential to our lives? Scholars in communication studies seem to concur on one thing and it is that

> the media do not tell us what to think or how to behave, but they do tell us what to think about. The media shape perceptions. The stories told through the media constitute a variety of frames, or to change the metaphor, a multitude of mirrors, which reflect back to us a variety of, more or less distorted, images of our world. In a pluralistic society especially, the media tell many stories from many different and often contradictory, perspectives. This then raises the question of who is telling the stories (and by what authority) and the related issues of what stories are being told what values they contain and how they are being received.[31]

Before we glimpse how media is able to do what it does, the effect of media is best portrayed in two important examples. One example is from coverage during the Gulf War and the other more recently in 2003 involving the Iraqi War. Chris Arthur points out that Americans pride themselves on living in a society where "the unquestioned assumption [is] that there is a completely open, free flow of information." There was nothing free flowing about this orchestrated dissemination of choreographed information, as shown by Project Censored.

Project Censored, an organization that tries to identify and publicize stories on important issues that have been overlooked or underreported, announced that the Gulf War issues dominated the censored news list for 1991. For example, topping the list was the story that revealed how news departments at CBS and NBC rejected rare, uncensored footage taken at the height of the air war by two Emmy Award–winning documentary producers. The footage substantially contradicted U.S. administration claims that civilian damage from the American-led bombing campaign was light.[32]

> Righteous indignation flooded the hearts and minds of Americans when hearing that Iraqi soldiers had stormed Kuwaiti hospitals confiscating incubators and leaving newborn infants to die. Even George Bush referred to this incident in several of his speeches. The source of this information was an anonymous young Kuwaiti refugee who had testified to the alleged atrocities before a Congressional caucus. As it turned out, the young woman was the daughter of the Kuwaiti ambassador to the United States and had been coached and rehearsed before video cameras by the public relations firm of Hill and Knowlton, on behalf of their client, Citizens for a Free Kuwait, apparently funded by the Emir of Kuwait. Further investigation by news networks and interviews of Kuwaiti doctors indicated that no such incident had occurred.[33]

Even in the face of previous failure to perpetrate a lie by the first Bush administration, the second Bush administration tried the same tactics again in 2003. Americans were mesmerized and horrified by the capture of Private Jessica Lynch, her rape and torture, and her obvious resulting physical damage in Iraq. This story was so big that alarms were raised everywhere as media pundits used this series of events to confirm the viciousness, immorality, and lawlessness of Iraqis. Lynch signed a movie deal, and people in her home state of West Virginia marched, put up ribbons, and then prepared to welcome her home with great fanfare after her release. In fact the daring rescue of Private Lynch was another media-staging of a film short. BBC News (world edition) on Thursday May 15, 2003, asserted:

> Private Jessica Lynch became an icon of the war, and the story of her capture by the Iraqis and her rescue by U.S. Special Forces became one of the great patriotic moments of the conflict. But her story is one of the most stunning pieces of news management ever conceived.

Reports claimed she had stab and bullet wounds and that she had been slapped about on her hospital bed and interrogated.[34] In fact after the rescue and after Private Lynch had been taken to the hospital, a full "eight days later U.S. special forces stormed the hospital, capturing the 'dramatic' events on a night vision camera." In reality, she had injuries, consistent with an auto accident—broken bones. She had not been wounded by gunfire and had not been raped. Ironically, her return to U.S. protection was stopped by U.S. forces who fired on the ambulance that carried her. Now that the U.S. government has taken propaganda to a new level and is backed up by both the movie industry and media, what is scripted for Americans to know is increasingly suspect.

So now we are better informed as to why the story of Muslim immigrants in the United States, according to many sources, has largely been the collective stories of Arab Muslims in the United States. We are also better informed on how various forms of knowledge have converged and painted a particular picture of Islam and Muslims. Even though we know (because the newspapers and magazines have told us) that the largest, single ethnic group of American Muslims is African American and that the largest group of immigrant Muslims is South Asian, there is the persistence of our old syllogism—all the Arabs are Muslim and all the Muslims are Arab. Now we know how this particular group of Muslims (the Arabs who are indeed Muslim and not Christian) came to be stereotyped in a particular denigrating way both by their own efforts and those of our government. Media also has sounded other alarms regarding Islam and Muslims.

Following the Oklahoma City bombing on April 19, 1995, when terrorist experts and news reporters were on television decrying the fact that those who were responsible were Muslims, there were over two hundred reports of anti-Muslim violence and harassment in just a few days.[35] Of the victims reporting these incidents 45 percent were Arab and 17 percent were South Asian. An apology was never given the general American Muslim community even in the face of the arrest, conviction, and execution of Timothy McVeigh.

After media coverage of TWA's Flight 800 crash on July 17, 1996, Muslims again, and predominantly Arab Muslims, experienced immediate threats of violence. Although Muslims were not involved in either of these incidents, broadcasters insisted on associating these events with acts of terrorism in the Middle East. Discriminations regarding observance of religious practices, employment, searches and seizures of both person and dwelling, and detainments of persons of Arab background on suspicion of aiding "terrorist" organizations are just a portion of the new realities of Arabic-speaking Americans. Mosques are especially vulnerable to attack. In June 1996 the Islamic Center of Northern Virginia in Fairfax was vandalized; the mosque in West Springfield, Massachusetts, was attacked in October 1996; criminals attacked the Islamic Center of West Virginia in December 1996. CAIR, the Council on American-Islamic Relations, reported more than one thousand incidents of harassment or hate crimes against Muslims in 2003. CAIR reports in 2004:

> Last year marked the highest number of Muslim civil rights cases ever recorded by CAIR's annual report on the status of Muslim civil rights in the United States. Reports of harassment, violence and discriminatory treatment increased nearly 70 percent over 2002 (the year after the 9/11 terror attacks). This represents a three-fold increase since the reporting year preceding the terrorist attacks.

Although reports of abuse in areas of passenger profiling and unreasonable arrest, search and seizure have dropped significantly, incidents of hate crime have more than doubled. Also, allegations of mistreatment by federal and local law enforcement personnel (including profiling and discriminatory application of the law) accounted for a third of all reports, the highest record ever in real and proportionate terms.[36]

BBC online service for June 26, 2002, asserted:

> As part of the war on terror, the U.S. intends to fingerprint and photograph tens of thousands of visitors and build up databases on individuals, especially Arabs and Muslims, known as "profiling."

The authorities cannot build databases on all 35 million visitors who enter the U.S. annually. So, privately they admit they will be focusing on Arabs.

How can we finally explore the lives of immigrant American Muslims without the layers of constructed images and stereotypes? One possible beginning is through a brief examination of the distinctions in American culture and some of the various American Muslim cultures.

3

Brief Introduction to Islam

The private and public lives of Muslims in America are often a continuing series of calibrations between work, entertainment, family demands, and the disciplines of Islam. Evening pastimes such as watching television are spaced around prayer times. Ramadan, the month of fasting/restraint, is based on a lunar calendar, so the dates change every year. Practicing Muslims often find themselves fasting while working and/or studying. Muslims also have to calculate two "taxes" on their income and holdings. There are two obligations every year, one payment for the IRS and the other for *zakat* (a purification of wealth) at the end of Ramadan. Readers can imagine the dilemma no matter which occurs first. For most American Muslims there are no voices chanting the call to prayer from minarets at the neighborhood *masajid* (mosques, pl.) five times daily; there is prayer and restraint in a sea of cable/satellite stations, overeating, and public sexuality.

As mentioned previously, non-Muslim Americans see very little of the private lives of Muslims, and are fed carefully constructed media views of both Islam and Muslim that are devoid of the religious life. In survey after survey, non-Muslim Americans invariably claim to know little about either Islam or Muslims. Islam in modern America is almost a century old and members of its community number in the millions.[1] Newspapers, magazines, TV news programs and talk shows write and report the most outlandish stories about Islam and Muslims, without counter-balanced reports of contributions Muslims make to the United States, especially in critical areas such as medicine and engineering. Islam is almost palpable, yet really still invisible despite being portrayed as a direct threat to Americans and, thus, to the world. Nevertheless, enduring questions for most intellectually curious Americans are—What is Islam and who are Muslims? The most infamous and elusive Muslim in the world today is Osama bin Laden, who is portrayed as both an evil genius and a mindless idiot. At once he is the head of a global criminal enterprise that rivals the resources and power of many nations and is stupid enough to leave a mountain of evidence behind him. At least since the Iranian Revolution in 1979 and notably since the fall of the Soviet Union, Muslims have been suspect citizens often considered aliens, and since September 11, 2001, all Muslims have been guilty of conspiring to wage war against the freedom and security of the United States.[2] Recently the

United States government has taken great pains to publicly characterize Islam as a religion of peace while simultaneously calling Islam a religion of violence. What is Islam?

Islam—the Essentials

Islam is an Arabic word that connotes the peace of being that ensues from the submission of the human will to the will of God. Muslims are those who seek to submit their will to the will of God. Those people who begin the process of submission by attesting that "There is no god, but Allah and Muhammad is his messenger," are legally Muslims, that is, they are obligated to follow Islamic law and receive its benefits. The Qur'an is the culmination of a long series of revelations (twenty-three years) from Allah to the human community through the prophet Muhammad and the message is universal, calling humans to worship God and God alone. This is the primordial reference of Islam, which every prophet since Adam has brought to the human community. The historical or local Islam arose with the last revelation of God to the prophet Muhammad in seventh-century Arabia.

At the center of Islam sits the revelation—The Qur'an. It is a recitation, and its written text is called a *mushaf.* Daily memorization and recitation keep its contents alive in the human community. The contents provide a history of creation of this universe from God's point of view, that is, a history of the struggle of humans to submit their will to the will of God. It also provides a series of disciplines for submitting the will, guidance for societal relations, and guidance in dealing with people of other faiths. The Qur'an has 114 *suras* (fenced enclosures) whose smallest units are *ayat* (signs, pl.).[3] Muslims believe that the Qur'an is the verbatim word of God without mediation, impressed upon the heart of the prophet Muhammad (May peace and blessings be upon him, abbreviated—pbuh [peace be upon him]) by the angel Jibril (Gabriel) in seventh-century Arabia, over a period of twenty-three years.

The *suras* vary in length and are not recited or read in the chronological order of the revelation but rather in an order given in a revelation to the prophet Muhammad (pbuh). Each *sura* is named and numbered for reference. Allah says in the Qur'an that he will protect it from error, and Muslims have for fourteen centuries committed it to memory to add a human layer of protection. This has been one safeguard against deviation in its recitation (in one or more of ten approved dialects, the dialects of Arabia at the time of revelation) or its words. Any translation of the Qur'an is just that, a translation, it is not the Qur'an. Only the Qur'an in the Arabic of revelation is the Qur'an. For the Bedouin of Arabia who first heard it, it challenged everything they knew to be true. The

Qur'an compels its hearers to examine their lives, understand their potentialities, to become aware of the successes and failures of communities before them. Its audiences are asked to observe God's signs in the universe, to comprehend that this world will come to an end and that they will be held responsible and accountable for their actions in this life, and finally, through the revelation, they will know that there is only one God who is merciful and just.

The Prophet Muhammad (pbuh)

The prophet Muhammad (pbuh) was the last in a long series of prophets and messengers sent to human communities with the message of the existence of God and the obligation of humans to strive to submit their will to the will of God. This last message was universal in scope and represents the final warning to humankind. Evidence of a constant message is seen throughout the traditions of the world in their moral/ethical codes and in their articulations of the impermanence of this life and the fragility of human successes. The prophet Muhammad (pbuh) also had a complicated role in delivering the message.[4] Muhammad ibn Abdullah was born in seventh-century Arabia. It is asserted that he was destined to be a spiritual, social, and political leader; he is a model for Muslims. He was a father, husband, and prophet. The prophet Muhammad (pbuh) broke with the traditions of his tribe and ancestors as he set the example of how the worldview of the Qur'an is to be lived. As head of both a religious community and a state, he was the sole religious authority as well as a politician. His conduct and sayings were remembered by those closest to him, and have been studiously passed on to each successive generation.

Muslims have a huge body of texts detailing the life and work of the Prophet (pbuh) called *Sira*, *Sirat ar-rasul*, "the Conduct/Life of the Prophet." *Sirat ar-rasul* forms the basis of the *Sunna* (tradition). These are the reported conversations with the Prophet (pbuh) and observations of his behavior, and they form the basis of another series of texts called *Hadith* literature. These reports, authenticated by a number of firsthand witnesses whose names are recorded with the report and whose biographies are kept in a separate series of texts, form the set of references for Muslim behavior. Thus every Muslim has access to both the wisdom behind, and the "how to" of, the Prophet (pbuh) as Allah made him the guide for the community in both private and public behavior. Because the prophet Muhammad (pbuh) could not write, scribes immediately recorded what he received in revelation. In addition Arabia's literacy was stored in its oral tradition and in its vehicle, the prodigious memory of the Arabs. By the written record and by their recitation of the verbatim record, the revelation was protected and preserved.[5]

The man who became the prophet Muhammad (pbuh) was born in the city of Mecca into a respected though not wealthy clan. His father, Abdallah, died before his birth and his mother died while he was a child. Old Arabian tradition dictated that babies born in the city should be nurtured in the desert among the Bedouin where they could develop the endurance, strength, courage, and loyalty necessary to survive in the land. This is what Aminah, Muhammad's mother, provided for him by giving him to a wet nurse by the name of Halimah. Returning to Mecca after his weaning, the orphaned Muhammad was given to the care of his uncle. He developed through a livelihood of commerce into an adult renowned for his truthfulness, commercial skills, and honesty.

His commercial and social reputation along with his values, instilled in the desert, brought him to the attention of a wealthy, previously married, financially successful, widowed mother who was fifteen years his senior. Her name was Khadijah bint Khuwaylid. Khadijah hired Muhammad to manage her caravan business. After a time she was successful in a proposal of marriage to him. Khadijah bint Khuwaylid was the first follower of Islam. She was also, as his wife, a contributor to the Prophet (pbuh) and the early Muslim community. Their marriage lasted for fifteen years. Their union produced four daughters—Fatimah, Ruqqayah, Umm Khulthum, and Zaynab added to her at least three children from previous marriages. Two sons died in infancy—al-Qasim and Abdallah. Khadijah died shortly after the prophet Muhammad (pbuh) began to receive revelation.[6] At her death Muhammad (pbuh) found himself a prophet, single parent, and leader of a small community. It remained so for the first ten years of revelation.[7] Muhammad's marriage to Khadijah however, was not his only marriage. He later married multiple times to women in all stations of life—a virgin girl, widow, and divorcees—one the divorced wife of an ex-slave. Included in these marriages were a Jew and a Christian from different tribes. These marriages cemented tribal loyalties across religious and ethnic boundaries and provided an example for new configurations of loyalty and community. His marriages taught Muslims that they could and should marry widows, and divorced women, thus breaking with long-held traditional tribal taboos.

The message of Islam came into a region where, although both Judaism and Christianity (in its Monophysite version) were known, polytheism was the largest tradition. Meccans and other Arabs had a great number of gods they worshipped whose symbols were housed in the Ka'ba.[8] The message of submission to the one God and the critique of both Judaism and Christianity made the young Muslim community a threat to the existing order. The Qur'anic assertions on the equality of women, the Day of Judgment, a life after death, and the command to stand against injustice, disrupted Meccan society. Meccan society had no understanding of accountability outside the individual tribe. There were no notions of an afterlife. Continuous death threats and violence in Mecca against the Muslims led to a decision to emigrate. The opportunity for it arose when the people of Yathrib (now known as Medina) sought out a trusted person to settle their civil war. They sought out the prophet Muhammad (pbuh) and solicited his assistance. He agreed to move his community to Medina only if it would be protected and allowed to flourish.

This demand was granted, and Yathrib became the first Islamic city-state. As a political leader, the prophet Muhammad (pbuh), with the guidance of the Qur'an, built a city-state based on an understanding that the ultimate arbiter and source of authority is God. He established this understanding in a constitution. Revelation continued for almost ten more years.

> Islam provided an economic, social and political system, the Pax Islamica. Of this system, religion was as integral part, since it provided the ideas on which the whole was based. The peace and security under the system were the "security of God and of His Messenger."[9]

The prophet Muhammad's (pbuh) success was extraordinary in transforming both the spiritual and political life of seventh-century Arabia. Yet even more astounding was the consolidation of beliefs and practices of the nascent community.

Beliefs and Practices

Islamic beliefs follow the fundamental assertions of the Qur'an. *Tawhid*, literally "you be aware of the oneness" of God, is the centerpiece of the primordial message and thus of the Qur'an. There is no god but Allah. God is the only entity worthy of worship and this fact should influence humans to act in certain ways. Muslims engage this concept by placing a high value on morality, achievement, accountability, and responsibility. The greatest disobedience in Islam is to associate anything with God. The relationship between humans and God in Islam is one of obedience or disobedience. Humans are fully accountable and responsible for whether or not they decide to be obedient. It is important to note here that *tawhid* is the pivot around which everything in Islam revolves. In the Islamic worldview, the human is born innocent until reaching the age of discernment (usually puberty) where (s)he can make choices about right and wrong. Qur'anic Arabic and the notions of *tawhid* and of human innocence provide the glue for the culturally diverse Islamic community.

In the Qur'an the creation of humanity in this universe was a deliberate act made known to other creations of God—such as angels (creations of light, without will) and to the shaitan (creation of fire with will like humans). God created angels to be absolutely obedient to him. One of their many tasks has always been to deliver revelation from God to the various prophets and messengers. In the Qur'an they also serve as recorders of human deeds, agents of God in his relationship with humans, and heralders of the Day of Judgment.

As mentioned previously, the Qur'an is the last of a series of revelations sent via prophets to humankind. Muslims believe this and it follows that they also believe in the messages sent to those prophets before the advent of the last prophet, Muhammad (pbuh). Muslims learn that every prophet from Adam to Muhammad brought the same essential message of *tawhid.* In the West, where there is acknowledgment of a limited number of prophets, the notion of Abrahamic faiths describes the similarities between Judaism, Christianity, and Islam. This notion however, is not as broad a look at history as the Qur'anic view where the number of prophets is extensive, linking all the revelations they received to the primordial message. Nevertheless, it is the Qur'anic assertion of a line of prophets that, in theory, prevents in Islam much of the animosity between religious communities. For Muslims all the prophets—Adam, Noah, Lot, Moses, Jesus, and Muhammad (pbuh) are messengers of God.

Accordingly, since history and the future in the Qur'an are told from God's point of view, Muslims believe in the primordial nature of the Qur'an and the fact that God has given each human community knowledge of his will through messengers and prophets. There is also an understanding that some of the more recent of these scriptures—the *Torat* (Torah), *Injil* (Gospel)—have been tampered with and/or distorted as they passed from generation to generation. Nonetheless, because these communities received revelation, Jews and Christians have a special status according to the Qur'an—they are "people of the Book."

The Qur'an states, and Muslims believe, that there is a "measure for everything." Examples such as seasons, the rotations of the sun and moon, even the changes in cultures are evidence of this "measure." Coupled with the concept of a "measure" is the fact that God is all-powerful, all-seeing, all-knowing—everything has a measure. Thus, while God knows the beginning and ending of each thing in creation, humans have will, and on the level at which humanity functions in creation, they have choices. Human choice, however, does not preclude God's knowing. Thus Muslims believe that everything in creation has a fixed time for existence confirming God's omnipotence and omniscience.

Not the least of concerns is a belief in the Day of Judgment. This belief, after the belief in one God, explains the purpose of all actions in the Islamic worldview. The Qur'an points to the Day of Judgment as one endtime—earthly existence ends but eternity (real time) begins. Each individual life, we know, has an end, and the life of all of creation has an end. On the Day of Judgment, humans (everyone since the beginning of time) will be held accountable and responsible for their obedience and/or disobedience to the will of God. This is the message that the prophet Muhammad (pbuh) received, and then his companions dispersed themselves throughout the civilized and uncivilized world in the seventh-century.

The Expansion of Islam

After the death of the prophet Muhammad (pbuh), the community of Believers experienced a five-year period of intense communal conflict and development. The Prophet's (pbuh) death raised to a level of criticality the issue of leadership. Several claims on leadership were asserted from quite a few quarters. Eventually one set of claims emerged and became predominant. One group, those who felt that the Prophet's cousin and son-in-law ʿAli was the natural successor and the one named by the Prophet (pbuh), became known as Shiat ʿAli (also known as Shiʿites or Shiʿa). This group went on to form one major religious branch in Islam. The majority of the companions preferred Abu Bakr, one of the oldest and most loyal early followers of the Prophet (pbuh) and his father-in-law. Abu Bakr became the first of the commanders of the community of Believers *(amir al-muʿminin).* His reign, cut short by death, lasted two years and was followed by that of ʿUmar ibn al-Khattab (r. 634–644) who continued the push for expansion and order. The third khalifa (ruler of the Muslims), was Uthman ibn Affan (r. 644–656), who proved an ambiguous figure in Islamic history. Many scholars cite corruption and nepotism as his major faults but all acknowledge the expansion of the Islamic empire during his reign. Finally, after twenty-four years, ʿAli did become the khalifa, inheriting the unrest and conflict of Uthman's leadership and new challenges to governance. The horrific murders of ʿAli and, later, one of his sons, Husayn, consolidated his supporters as a formal *Shiat ʿAli* (the party of ʿAli, Shiʿite Muslims).

Shiat ʿAli was only one of the "new" Muslim communities that emerged after the death of the Prophet (pbuh). For the party of ʿAli, governance lay in the family of the prophet Muhammad (pbuh). According to this understanding, Allah did not leave the community without direct guidance after the death of the Prophet pbuh). This guidance held that direct kin relationship to the family of the Prophet (pbuh) was a prerequisite of leadership. The majority of Muslims (Sunni) held that the notion that the consensus of the community of learned believers was the most important element in establishing a legitimate claim to lead the Muslim community—forming the basic idea of governance in Sunni Islam. In Sunni Islam guidance for the community is derived from the Qurʾan and *Hadith* literature by the learned in the community. These two notions of leadership have prevailed in the Muslim world—Shiʿite, Sunni—and emigrated with the nascent Arab Muslim community as it moved out of Arabia in the seventh century. Issues of leadership and relations within the community were paramount and remain so today.

The Muslim world moved eastward out along the Silk Road through India, China, and what would become the former Soviet Union. It consumed all of Egypt and moved across North Africa, maintaining the same criteria for leadership. Although Sufism begins early in Muslim life, it was not until the late seventeenth and early eighteenth centuries, with the organization of Sufi Muslim communities (proponents of mysticism) that a new pattern of leadership emerged to support Islam especially in regions removed from the Arab center such as China and the Russian states. While the traditional understandings of authority had come to rest in the law, Sufism offered a parallel focus and a space for individual religiosity.[10] Many modern scholars attribute the rapid growth of Sufism to the stultifying effect of strict adherence to the law demanded by Sunni scholars. Clearly, part of the reason for the insistence on the law was aimed at keeping a codified set of beliefs and practices in the growing Muslim community. While Sufism did not change the fundamental/essential beliefs and practices, it did change the locus of authority, in most cases adding to the practices. One conspicuous addition was the notion that Muslims could cleanse themselves spiritually in such a way as to make themselves pure enough to be available for revelation as the prophet Muhammad (pbuh) was when the angel Jibril was sent to him.

Since both Sunni and Shiʿa incorporated Sufi practices into Islam, it became part of the public and private order in Muslim communities, but the law predominates. The ideas of "right practice"—orthopraxy, maintained a tension throughout much of the Arab and South Asian world and do so today. The *Shariʿah*, commonly known as Islamic Law became the province of a learned few, and those few held sway over community life and relationships. History records over five hundred schools of Islamic law that eliminated each other until there were four agreed upon schools in Sunni Islam and one predominant school in Shiʿa Islam. Sunni Islam is the dominant branch of Islam and the four surviving schools traveled to distant lands with one school predominating in each region with exceptions of Shiʿa Islam's Jafari School, which predominates in Iran. Though one may think that Islamic law made each new Muslim community look just like the community of Arabia, it did not, as new communities kept their ethnic traditions.

Cultures that embraced Islam did not relinquish all of their traditions, only those that were patently in opposition to the main tenets of Islam such as polytheism, drinking alcohol, or eating pork. Other traditions such as praying at the graves of ancestors, asking for intercession from those "known to have gifts from God," marriage ceremonies, or the traditional treatment of women, were not affected by the adoption of Islam. Arab traditions, assumed to be religiously legitimate, were added to existing traditions.[11] This collage of Arab (and thus presumed Islamic, since all things Arab are not Islamic) traditions and cultural traditions make up what is the Muslim world. Muslims often speak of the difference between Islam and culture, though they vigorously practice both, with culture often taking precedence. Nevertheless, from the village of Medina in seventh-century Arabia, Muslims created an outstanding civilization.

To get a clear picture of the diversity of cultures that adopted Islam either totally or partially, the reader must refer to a map. Within ten years of the Prophet's (pbuh) death, Arab Muslims conquered what is present day Iraq, Syria, Palestine, and Egypt along with the western portion of Persia. Arab ships by 720 C.E. landed and overtook Cyprus, Carthage, Tunis, Gibraltar, Spain, southern France to the west, and the Hindu-Buddhist society of Sind. They met the Chinese armies in 651 C.E.

> Thus within 130 years of Islam's birth, Arab armies and navies had conquered a broad swath of the known world from Gibraltar to the Indus delta, and had penetrated both China and Europe by land and sea.[12]

Arab Muslims, like countless others before them, engaged "new" Muslims and their knowledge for the benefit of the expanse of the emerging civilization and in return gave them the Arabic language and traditions. Muslims in various parts of the Islamic world contributed to the world in literature, philosophy, and architecture. Persian Muslims contributed their ancient art forms, music, philosophy, medicinal knowledge, and so on to this civilization. Central Asian Muslims gave their knowledge of textiles, papermaking, inks, and dyes. As Muslims translated the medical and philosophical works of the Greeks into Arabic, added to them, and made them once again available to the world, Arabic words became a part of several western languages. Islamic civilization was in many respects an age of enlightenment for the known world. Muslims wrote some of the earliest essays in comparative religion; for example, Abu Muhammad ʿAli ibn Hazm's (456 C.E.) *Book of Religion and Sects*. They also wrote compendiums of pharmacology and medicine.[13]

Ar-Razi in the tenth century distinguished for the first time between smallpox and measles and was also the first person to identify hay fever and discover its cause. Abu ʿAli al-Husayn ibn ʿAbd Allah ibn Sina, known in the West as Avicenna, was one of the great intellectuals. He wrote an encyclopedia of medicine that was used in the Muslim world until the nineteenth century and in Europe until the seventeenth century.[14] He was the first to describe and identify meningitis. He recommended alcohol as a disinfectant and wrote at least twenty books of theology, metaphysics, poetry, and astronomy. Other Muslims advanced knowledge in mathematics and physics. When Muslims speak of a glorious past they are referring not only to the ascendancy of Islamic rule but also to centuries of discoveries and cooperation with non-Muslims in fields of medicine, mathematics, astronomy, and literature. Many historians date the beginning of the decline in Islamic civilization to the end of the twelfth century, and its unquestionable fall at the end of the seventeenth century. This long period of decline made the decay almost invisible to the large populations of the various cultures that made up the Muslim world.

Though faith in Islam is never blind, corrupt rulers have kept vast portions of the Muslim world oppressed and illiterate since the eighteenth century. Even as Islamic civilization produced some of the most important discoveries in astronomy, medicine, and so on, the majority population has never engaged itself in the pursuit of knowledge, either of the Qur'an itself or of the world. This fact is one underlying contributor to the end of Muslim dominance in the world that began with European industrialization and modernization in the eighteenth century. Differences in leadership styles, unresolved conflicts such as the Shi'a and Sunni disputes, a corrupt and petty series of rulers, and a large illiterate population, in predominantly agrarian societies all contributed to the Muslim world's inability to keep pace with industrialization or even to begin their own forms of modernization. The dissonance formed by the existence of several Muslim empires simultaneously also contributed to their colonization by Europe. By the beginning of the twentieth century, European nations had dismantled the last of the Muslim empires, chopped a contiguous nation into nation-states and were able to do so without concerted, unified protests from anywhere in the Muslim world.

Muslims had for centuries lived in a world where travel was limited only by one's personal resources. There were, of course, boundaries, but the empires were ruled from one central place. The last Islamic empire was the Ottoman Empire, which was dismantled in 1924, enabling the creation of Syria, Lebanon, Palestine, and Iraq. European colonization had also restructured Africa into new states and thus, new nationalities. The impact of this colonialization and subsequent neocolonialization is still present throughout the Muslim world in every sector of life. In the absence of empire, Muslims have immortalized those centuries of prosperity and have sought from theology, history, and philosophy the answers to their current state of chaos. Maintaining the *ummah* (community of believers) is primary, and there is much confusion over what caused the decline and how to move forward with their own agenda for modernization.

Much of the pain and suffering is felt economically, resulting in migrations to the West.

The Presence of Islam

The Great Mosque and the Ka'ba in Mecca, Saudi Arabia, are keys to Islam's spiritual geography.[15] Five times daily, Muslims all over the world wash themselves and turn to face the Ka'ba in Saudi Arabia—turning to the *Qibla.*[16] *Believers first check the direction of the Qibla* from the space where they are going to pray. Once the direction has been established, the prayer begins.

> We see you turning your face (for guidance) to the heavens: now will we turn you to a Qibla that will please you. Turn then your face in the direction of the Sacred Mosque: wherever you are, turn your faces in that direction. The Qur'an 2:144.

The first *masjid* (mosque, sing.) was that of the Prophet(pbuh), built in Medina in the year 1 A.H. (after the *hijra*).[17] A *masjid* is a place of prostration where Muslims gather to pray, although they may pray alone or with others, at home or elsewhere. The *masjid* became a physical symbol of Islam early in Islamic history. It usually houses a school called a *madrassah* where religious instruction is given. The call to prayer for the community is recited five times daily from a tower called a minaret. Inside the *masjid*, the focal point is called the *mithrab*—showing the direction of the *Qibla.* Friday (*Jum'ah*) is the day of congregational prayer—*salat al-jumu'a,* which is held instead of the midday prayer. This prayer is accompanied by an important instructive and moral talk, *khutba,* given by the leader of the prayer—imam (who is the most knowledgeable in the Qur'an).

> O you who believe! When the call is proclaimed to prayer on Friday, hasten earnestly to the remembrance of Allah, and leave off business that is best for you if you but knew. The Qur'an 62:9

This is not a day of worship in the tradition of a Sabbath, rather it is a period of time, from twenty minutes to an hour, after which Muslims are to return to work. There is not an understanding in Islam of a Sabbath day.

The Qur'an and Islamic law also proscribe dietary restrictions for Muslims.

> Forbidden to you (for food) are dead meat, blood, the flesh of swine, and that on which has been invoked the name of other than Allah; that which has been killed by strangling, or by a violent blow, or by a headlong fall,

> or by being gored to death; that which has been (partly) eaten by a wild animal, unless you are able to slaughter it; that which is sacrificed on stone (altars). The Qur'an 5:3

The process by which meat is rendered *halal* (permissible) is called *zabiha.* Muslims, especially those living in the West, have published books on foods that are permissible since the largely Christian West uses many pork products in food preservation and as ingredients. Response to this dilemma is the opening, in many cities, of *halal* grocery stores where Muslims can shop without concern.

The Muslim calendar (the era of the *hijra*) is built on the lunar year. This calendar begins on September 24, 622 C.E. and is labeled 1 A.H., which corresponds to the twelfth day of the Islamic month, *Rabi' al-Awwal.* The Muslim year is a lunar year consisting of twelve months, which are twenty-nine or thirty days long. It has 355 or 356 days, a difference of about eleven days from the solar year. The first month is *Muharram* and the last month is *Dhu'l Hijja,* which is also the month of the pilgrimage to Mecca. Muslims living in different parts of the world have cultural holidays but all Muslims celebrate two—*'Id al-fitr* and *'Id al-Adha. 'Id al-fitr* is the feast celebrating the breaking of the fast of Ramadan.[18] *'Id al-Adha* occurs on the tenth day of *Dhu'l Hijja* and commemorates the prophet Abraham's willingness to sacrifice his son Ismail on Allah's command. This sacrifice, celebrated by Muslims around the world, is at the end of the pilgrimage in Mecca. Charity and sharing are at the center of this celebration. Sheep are slaughtered and eaten with a portion or another whole sheep slaughtered to give to the poor. These two celebrations, practiced by all Muslims, along with the disciplines of belief are not the only things that make Muslims a community. Additionally, there are behaviors advised by the Qur'an and some reported by the writers of *Hadith* literature.

The Qur'an instructs all Muslims, regardless of gender, to be modest (not exaggerated) in dress, manner, and speech. Muslims are to always be aware of the time for prayer and vigilant about the environments into which they put themselves. Every believer greets another with the salutation, *as salaamu alaikum!*—may peace be with you. And every believer responds to this greeting with *wa alaikum salaam!* (and may peace be on you!). Muslims learn to perform "good" acts, such as eating, with the right hand, and necessary but potentially polluting acts, such as cleaning out their nostrils, with the left hand. The language of the Qur'an is woven into everyday speech, such as when a Muslim utters a plan for something like going somewhere the statement is followed by *inshallah* (if Allah wills it). This keeps in mind that she or he is not in control of the outcome of actions. The list of behaviors extends to personal hygiene, sexual relations, contractual relations, prayer, and so on. Despite its multiplicity of cultures, Islam has evolved common patterns of behavior in addition to beliefs and practices that make for a worldwide community—the *ummah*.

Summary

The first eleven centuries of Islam spawned a dynamic multicultural civilization from southern France across to the Far East. We can call this the topside, where art and science flourished and dynasties were built and nurtured. On the underside however, in a symbiotic relationship, economic disparity, mistreatment of women, misinterpretation of Qur'anic exhortations and admonitions by those in leadership, and a culture of illiteracy grew at the same pace. As mentioned earlier, those cultures that adopted Islam did so without much change in fundamental cultural values, though if the Qur'anic guidance had been implemented, many of these cultural mores would have been extinguished.

To understand Islam today, the researcher should first ascertain the societal vision in the Qur'an itself. Humankind is created with will and to serve God and God alone. Humans are given knowledge of things and are to spend time discovering the signs of God in nature, how things work in synergy, and how best to derive what is necessary for human growth and development without destruction. The focus in the Qur'an is on "believers" and their behaviors and acts. These behaviors and acts are spelled out with reference to the behavior and acts of other communities. Muslims along with others who believe in God and God alone are rewarded for correct worship and acts. And Muslims along with others are punished for incorrect acts. The Qur'an gives apt descriptions of Paradise and Hell. What is present on the underside is focused elsewhere.

As mentioned earlier, those cultures that adopted Islam did so without change in some fundamental relationships. Those Muslims who descended from the Prophet's (pbuh) line lay claims to "special favor" and though not always heirs to fortune, found fame. It is understood that these *as-Sayyid* are rigorous in study and righteousness. Knowledge of the Qur'an and the sayings of the Prophet also quickly formed a class of learned men. Learned women were quickly erased from bibliographies even though they were among the teachers of esteemed men.

Islam continued to spread after the Prophet's death. There emerged the problem of making sure the accurate message of the Qur'an spread with it. The community experienced its first real need for unity. The central question became how to make sure new Muslims held to Islamic standards. The *sahabah* (companions of the Prophet [pbuh]) were dying of old age, in wars and excursions, and moving separately with armies into new territories. Each new culture Arabs encountered posed different challenges. Without a consultative body or ready means of communication, it became imperative to codify the law. Initially, almost every *sahabah* becomes a source of authority. Each school used its own methods of deducing whether an act or utterance was permissible or not. In the end four schools survived the turmoil.

While the methods of jurisprudence are unique and exceptional in quality, the law's partial reliance on the narrations of the sayings and actions of the Prophet (pbuh) have been most challenging to women, the poor, and the concerns of societal development. While the Qur'an's emphasis is on the beliefs and actions of believers, (men and women; women and men), justice, and compassion are all but erased by its interpreters. Largely due to cultural norms, emphasis is placed on maintaining a curious patriarchal suppression of women and other family patterns, unjust relations with the poor, and maintaining great disparities in wealth. Qur'anic guidance on the structure of relationships between believers, husbands and wives, or neighbors is articulated but rarely practiced.

Muslims have struggled with these ambiguities and others for centuries. The last few centuries have demonstrated that the ambiguities have intensified to crisis proportions. Simultaneously, colonialism and then neocolonialism devastated almost every society in the Muslim world. As the wealth potentials of the already wealthy and new classes of wealth created by colonial powers grew, the misery of the masses naturally increased. In almost every Muslim country this misery was met with oppression. Explanation for societal chaos was sought in Qur'anic guidance. One problem that seems to have occurred here is that an extreme problem was answered by extremes.

Oppressions, suppressions by monarchs and presidents alike in the form of censorship of the press, detentions, killings, jailings, prohibition of certain associations, and the absence of civil rights rendered Muslim societies unable to develop. There are no truly traditional societies in the Muslim world. Every society has met the West in one form or another. Abilities to seize potential opportunities of any kind, however, are to a great extent a function of literacy and resources. While the West desires to replicate itself, turning every country into both a puppet state and a market economy, some Muslims find this offer a ploy for domination while others see it as a train toward self-actualization. Some of those in the second category who are both literate and with access to resources flee at the first opportunity. Others pool resources to enable someone in a family or village to escape in hopes that they will either rescue the others or send money back home to make life at least tolerable. Still others use the Qur'an to seek answers to the horrible conditions of their societies.

Those seeking better education, more freedoms, and wealth make up the majority of immigrant Muslims in America. Yet there are a series of issues that surround the notion of immigration in the Muslim mind. The concept of emigration in the Islamic worldview is a concrete and fundamental part of its history. The Prophet of Islam, Muhammad ibn Abdullah, lived in Mecca, Arabia, while receiving the first revelations for about ten turbulent years. Consistent with the history of previous prophets, the prophet Muhammad (pbuh) and his community of believers faced insults, threats, imprisonment, and isolation. Life in Mecca quickly became so difficult that the prophet Muhammad (pbuh) sent those who were being persecuted most severely to the Negus of Abyssinia. This temporary emigration (for the duration of the hostilities) in 615 C.E., is known as the first *hijra,* and its vagaries set the parameters for the concept of immigration and its legal possibilities in Islamic thought until today. As the persecution of the nascent community of Muslims continued to escalate, the need for migration loomed again on the horizon.

Shortly after the Muslims were sent to Abyssinia, the prophet Muhammad (pbuh) was approached by representatives from the town of Yathrib (later named Medina) a few hundred miles away to act as a mediator between two warring tribes. He agreed to do so if his family and followers could move with him; his community would be supported until they could make their own livelihood; and that they would immediately be given full citizenship. This was the final agreement, and the Muslims fled to Yathrib in 622 C.E. This major emigration officially marks the beginning of the Islamic lunar calendar. Those who helped make this move successful are known as *ansar,* while those who made the *hijra* are called *muhajirun.*

As one organizing principle in the Islamic worldview, the concept of *hijra* was much discussed in the early centuries of Islam. Initially these conversations centered around interpretations of those migrations of the first community. The first *hijra* entailed a physical movement to a safe place with a government who accepted the Muslims to live for a short time without any impediments to their Islamic practice. It is the second *hijra,* a more permanent move, which initiated the political and social practices of Islam with the Prophet (pbuh) as both the political and spiritual leader of the community. Before each move a pact, contract or agreement was in force. Neither place of immigration was under a government that at the time was hostile to the new community of Muslims. The first *hijra* did not entail an effort to remain in Abyssinia, while the second, permanent, move established Islam as the religion and its precepts as the government. In both these scenarios, the move was made after a contact with the leader of the place of immigration.

As Muslims spread Islam, they took over the governments they conquered and the notion of *hijra* became a discussion on whether other Muslims should join those in the new place to swell their numbers. This notion of *hijra* has always carried with it Muslim security. The modern aberration is Muslims voluntarily emigrating to non-Muslim lands without such assurances. Migrations for financial, educational and marriage reasons have always taken place in Islamic history, inside and outside of Muslim lands. Today, Muslims are fighting to stay not in Muslim lands but in hostile lands.

4

South Asian History in Overview

Scholars actually do provide a great deal of accurate information on India and the other smaller countries in South Asia. Many travelers, anthropologists, historians, and scholars of comparative religion have vested themselves in the study of an India that is unchanged by time. One scholar notes the view of many other scholars that "the Indian subcontinent has not changed over the course of human history. It houses one of the largest Muslim populations of any modern state and most of them are descendants of those converted to Islam during the seven centuries when it was the religion of the Northern Indian political elite."[1]

The Indian subcontinent does indeed have one of the largest populations of Muslims in the world. Its history has also documented millennia of human habitation. Just imagine, its population comprises almost one-fifth of the world's population. For most of its entire history, India has also been known as the home of almost unimaginable wealth and artifacts. By the seventh century, India had "a single complex system of political, ideological, economic and cultural relations and institutions."[2] One fact about India that is well known (so much so that it is a synonym) is its caste system, which includes color, profession, and class distinctions. Poverty as a synonym for South Asia is a recent addition to the world's vocabulary, coming in the twentieth century. Rarely do westerners think about the inherent ambiguity in the portrayals of a South Asia mired in poverty while simultaneously producing some of the best physicians, engineers, and computer technicians in the world. Some of the reasons are provided in a brief look at South Asian Islamic history.

Islamic history on the Indian subcontinent began in the eighth century with the Arab conquest of Sind. Islam spread in authority and gained converts with the Mamluks (slave soldiers of Turkish origin who rose to power). From the twelfth to the fourteenth centuries, Muslim authority gradually established itself over the entire Indian subcontinent and cemented itself with the Mogul dynasty, which lasted until the British came in the nineteenth century. It is alarming how quickly this very extraordinary civilization lost its status in the world when the British arrived. The British supplanted Indian institutions with their own, thus transforming educational systems and social life. They created an elite from the Hindu majority, leaving the Muslims, who had previously belonged to the ruling class, without any real power. It was the beginning of what would become the state of affairs throughout the Muslim world: presence in numbers, but no power. Commenting on Muslims in the secular republic of India, Wilfred Cantwell Smith asserts:

> The question of political power and social organization, so central to Islam, has in the past always been considered in yes-or-no terms. Muslims have either had political power or they have not. Never before have they shared it with others. Muslims in India had always been a minority but had had power.[3]

Although even many Muslim historians of the region have considered Mogul (Muslim) rule benevolent, the changes Islam brought to the predominately Hindu land were deeply resented. Islam brought shrines, cemeteries, and meat-eating to a society that cremated its dead, was vegetarian, and had its own shrines. Though this Hindu resentment of Muslims aided the British conquest of India, and Hindus probably saw an immediate reinstatement of their values as the logical result, the British had other long-term agendas. Long-held resentment of Muslim practices and British anointment of Hindu superiority are at the core of twentieth-century Hindu nationalism and suppression of Muslims, and subsequent Muslim resentment.

In an article written in 1908 for the *Atlantic Monthly*, Jabez T. Sunderland notes:

> When the British first appeared on the scene, India was one of the richest countries of the world. . . . The source of her wealth was largely her splendid manufactures. Her cotton goods, silk goods, shawls, Muslims of Dacca, brocades of Ahmedabad, rugs pottery of Scind, jewelry, metal work, lapidary work. . . . What has become of those manufactures? For the most part they are gone, destroyed. . . . What is the explanation? Great Britain wanted India's markets.[4]

Sunderland, an American, in this cautious appeal to Britain's consciousness and a direct attempt to inform Americans, lists six causes of India's impoverishments and famine at the beginning of the twentieth century. While we could sum it all up with one phrase—"the British came and conquered," it is important to quickly review this list. Sunderland states that "one cause of India's impoverishment is heavy taxation." Britain taxed Indian citizens at a rate more than twice that of British citizens, at a sum of one-third their already meager annual income (six dollars average per person in 1905). While many of us in the United States, now in the twenty-first century, pay one-third of our annual income in taxes, the base salary on which we pay is considerably more—not creating starvation, just inconvenience. For Indians at the dawn of the twentieth century, heavy taxation—especially on salt, which is necessary for health—caused severe malnourishment and death in addition to increased poverty. As mentioned previously, another cause of India's impoverishment was the destruction of her manufacturing as a direct result of British rule. A not so obvious but important third cause was "the enormous and wholly unnecessary cost of her government," which was really the cost of British administration. Almost all of the highest officials and civil servants throughout the entire Indian subcontinent were British.

Britain owned the manufacturing, the railroads, and the means of commerce. It controlled education and all of the public space. India also had the burden of the "enormously heavy military expenses of the British government." She [India] was forced to house the British military and thus participate in Britain's wars and campaigns to claim dominance. Sunderland asserts that India was drained of more than 460 million dollars in the nineteenth century by Britain, all from citizens making on the average six dollars per year. Perhaps the greatest wrong exercised, according to scholars, was the destruction of freedom. India was kept in "absolute subjection," without redress. Britain, however, was beyond reproach for its imperialism in the international community and thus beyond Sunderland's questions as well. One has to remember that at this time the Untied States was a potential but not yet realized power with limited global influence, while other European countries were themselves actively involved in imperialistic efforts around the world.

By 1941 the population of India was around 390 million. In a series of defenses against a tide of insurrections against British rule (including Gandhi's successful nonviolent movement, which included Muslims, against the burden of taxes on salt), Britain began to show vulnerability, too little, too late.[5] By early 1947 "the British simply declared that they would leave India in June 1948. . . . " Jawaharlal Nehru proclaimed India a new nation on August 15, 1948. Muslims comprised fully a quarter of India's citizenry on the eve of independence from Britain. Pakistan already was a country on August 14, 1947. Even in retreat, Britain continued its dominance over India because it had left a permanent stamp of British culture on the minds, infrastructures, and values. The British left the country in chaos with inappropriate appointments in local government and no attention to the potential strife. There was, for example, a Muslim administrator over Hindus in Hyderabad and a Hindu official over the Muslim majority in Kashmir. Having spent more than a century under despotic rule that decimated the population of its honored integrity, it is no wonder that the South Asians that American moviegoers saw were impoverished and chaotic.

The creation of the states of India, Pakistan, and later Bangladesh, was not, however, the only cause of the religious sectarian violence that has plagued the region, but that is not the focus of this chapter. For our purposes it is important to distinguish the Muslims of the region as they are—Shi'ite, Sunni, or other.

South Asian Shi'ite Communities—The Ithna-Asheri, the Isma'ili, and the Daudi (Dawoodi) Bohra Isma'ili

While this text discusses Shi'ite Islam more fully in the chapter on Iranian Muslims, some discussion of Shi'ite Islam is necessary here. Shi'ite Islam is the second largest branch of Islam. Emerging out of a dispute over succession to the prophet Muhammad (pbuh), Shi'ite communities are principally divided over the nature of leadership in the Muslim community after the death of the prophet Muhammad (pbuh). The foremost community of Shi'ites recognizes twelve imams and is called Ithna-Asheri or the Twelvers. Both Twelvers and Isma'lis are subjects of our study. In addition to the basic philosophical stances between Sunni and Shi'ite, there are differences in religious interpretation between Twelvers and Isma'ilis, but Isma'ili are predominantly South Asian. Shi'ite Islam in America has invested itself in a portion of the Indian community primarily in the presence of Isma'ili Shi'ite Muslims.

The Ithna-Asheri

Ithna-Asheri Muslims (Twelvers) are the dominant branch of Shi'ite Muslims, found mostly in Iran, Iraq, Bahrain, and Kuwait but also in South Asia. In India they comprise a significant portion of the Muslim population. Together with the Isma'ilis they make up between 15 and 20 percent of the Muslim population. In Pakistan, a predominately Sunni state, the number of Shi'ites is put at twelve million, centered mainly in the Punjab, in the Lahore region.[6] Shi'ite Muslims follow many of the same core beliefs and practices as Sunni Muslims described earlier. They believe in the Oneness of God, the Qur'an, that the prophet Muhammad (pbuh) was God's messenger, in the resurrection followed by the last judgment, and the basic requirements of prayer, fasting, pilgrimage, purification of wealth, and jihad. To these essential beliefs, Shi'ite Muslims add belief in God's justice and the Imamate.

> The Imamate is to some extent the consequence and the application of the principle of justice to the guidance of humankind. God, who created men, could not let them go to their perdition. That is why He sent them the Prophets, the last of who was Muhammad, to guide them along the path of justice and truth. But after the death of the last Prophet it was unthink-

> able that God in His wisdom should leave men to their own devices without there being, in every era, a spiritual guarantor, proof of the truth of the revelation, to direct the community: this is the Imam, the "Guide."[7]

Because of the special position of the Imam as the intermediary between men and God, he can not be elected by men. "He must fulfill certain conditions of principle, be perfectly learned in religious matters, be absolutely just and equitable, be perfect, free from any fault, be the most perfect man of his time."[8] Since 874 C.E. Shiʿite Muslims have been living in the age of the twelfth Imam, hence the name Twelvers. This Imam is believed still to be alive but in hiding to return at the end of time, bringing an era of truth and justice.

As mentioned earlier, Sunni Muslims add *Hadith* literature and the law to the Qurʾan for guidance. Shiʿite Muslims use a different set of traditions called the "Four Books." These are *What Suffices in the Knowledge of Religion, He Who Has No Jurist at His Disposal, The Correction of Doctrines, The Clear-Sighted View of the Divergences of Tradition.* Shiʿite tradition also differs from Sunni tradition in the law. Two notable differences better the position of women regarding inheritance and marriage. Though Shiʿite Muslims observe prayer, they differ in how those prayers are executed. The prayers are performed three times daily—before dawn, at midday and afternoon, and in the evening and night. To the call to prayer, they add the phrase, "I attest that ʿAli is close to God," twice. One other distinction and perhaps one of the most distinguishing aspects of Twelve-Imam Shiʿite Islam is the remembrance of the Battle of Karbala.

A brief description of the death of the prophet Muhammad (pbuh) and the contestations over succession is given in Chapter 3. So, here, we can continue where that description ends. The nephew and son-in-law of the Prophet (pbuh), ʿAli, had two sons—Hasan and Hussein (sometimes spelled Hussayn or Hosein). Hasan decided not to fight for leadership. His brother Hussein, however, refused to pledge allegiance to the new ruler. In the process of rebellion, kept from advancing by the opposing forces, he stopped at a place in the desert called Karbala. The last battle was fought in this place on the morning of 10 Muharram (the second month on the Islamic calendar). Hussein, the Prophet's (pbuh) grandson, was decapitated; his head taken to Kufa and then to Damascus. His body was trampled and buried on the spot where a mausoleum stands today. This event is reenacted every 10 Muharram in the streets where Twelve-Imam Shiʿite Muslims live. In Shiʿite communities there is an adage that says, "the martyrdom of Hussein has become the prototype of every struggle for justice, every suffering." Other Shiʿite Muslims lament Hussein's death but do not commemorate his martyrdom.

The Isma'ili

Isma'ili Muslims, unlike the Twelvers, recognize only seven imams. There are other differences as well between the two Shi'ite communities. Shi'ite Muslims have divided over which Imam was the last of the guides. Thus, there are Five-, Seven-, and Twelve-Imam Shi'ite. Each community is designated by the number of accepted Imams with the last one expected to return at the end of time.

> Moreover, the complexity of theological and practical religious differences among the immigrant Muslim community has been virtually incomprehensible not only to outside observers but also to many Muslims, who in their native countries have belonged to and thus been familiar with one particular school of thought.[9]
>
> These very efforts, however, many times have tended to obscure adequate recognition of the vibrant Shi'ite Muslim community that is equally engaged in providing religious centers and facilitating systems of organization to protect the Islamic identity of its members. Even the academic enterprise has been remiss; until recently little acknowledgment was made of Shi'ite realities or information provided about Shi'ite communities in this country or in their home countries in conferences and studies on Islam in the American context.[10]

Professor Sachedina asserts that it is "reasonable to assert that Shi'ites make up at least 30 percent of the total Muslim immigrant population of North America." This figure includes both Iranians and South Asians though the percentage of Isma'ilis is higher. He is also proud of the fact that,

> the independent nature of the *marji' al-taqlid* (centralized authority) and the self-generated and self-managed financial structure of the Shi'ite religious organization has made it possible for the community to organize its affairs independent of the control of Muslim governments in the Middle East. Thus the political or religious problems of some of the Islamic centers funded by such countries as Saudi Arabia or Libya do not exist for the Shi'ite community.[11]

The Isma'ilis' fundamental beliefs are

- That God Almighty is One;
- That the Holy Prophet Muhammad (pbuh) is the last and final Prophet;
- That the life hereafter is true and the Dooms-Day is certain;
- That after the demise of the Holy Prophet Muhammad (pbuh) the presence of the Imam is necessary in all ages to maintain the unity of faith of those who

believe in him and to give them guidance befitting the changing conditions of the time and developing human society;

- That such Imam must always be available to his followers and is responsible for their guidance always and everywhere on the surface of the earth;
- That every such Imam must be in a genealogical line of succession right from Hazrat Ali, the first Imam, on the principle of a formal appointment of each predecessor Imam to his successor Imam;
- That Hazrat Ali, the first Imam, received his appointment as Imam from the Holy Prophet Muhammad (pbuh); and
- The Imam's guidance on matters of faith is binding on the community.

Though Isma'ili Muslims emerged in 765 C.E., their present-day leadership materialized in 1840 in the person of the first Aga Khan, Hasan Ali Shah. He was a governor of a province in Iran who fled to India because of a failed coup to seize power in Iran. He began a dynasty and leadership over the Isma'ili in India, Pakistan, Africa, Syria, and here in the United States.

The Aga Khans claim direct descent from the prophet Muhammad (pbuh) through the Prophet's daughter Fatima, and for the last two centuries have been considered the imams of the over fifteen million Isma'ili Muslims. Historically, they were made up of both Persians and Arabs who comprised the Fatimid dynasty and built the world's first university—al-Azhar in Cairo, Egypt. As mentioned before, in the nineteenth century, their primary ethnicity changed as did their major geographic locations. Converts to Isma'ilism from all over the Indian subcontinent—Burma, Ceylon, Malaysia, and the Middle East—became the main ethnic communities of the Aga Khan's international network. Through their worship centers, called *jama'at khana,* Isma'ilis have been very successful in keeping their community cohesive and closed to outsiders. Many of their differences with other South Asians who claim Islam, both Twelvers and Sunni, however, are overridden by the cultural ethos of South Asia regarding commerce and professional relationships, though Isma'ilis never worship with other Muslims. This extremely wealthy community is a model of survival, priding itself on its ability to assimilate into any country in which they reside, making sure to contribute to the community in the area of social services, such as health clinics.

Karim Aga Khan, the current leader, by all measures an intellectually astute and thoughtful leader, has developed a number of institutions to keep Isma'ilis all over the world connected. He alone interprets the faith, thereby preventing divisions over philosophy. The orders for equal treatment of women as well as the encouragement of youth to excel come from the Aga Khan and thus are binding. Members of this community enjoy the cooperative spirit of community in the institutions designed to assist at every level. The Aga Khan Foundation gives scholarships to members for education. Women sit on boards of the community and are expected to be active. Because members of the community come from all over the world, there is a diversity of culture although almost all can trace their ancestry to South Asia. (Note: The United States is a second or third diaspora or a significant number of members in the South Asian community.)

This community has also moved toward a solution of training future leaders in communities in the United States by establishing a religious school in Medina, New York and in Chicago for both young men and women. The Isma'ili community has been enormously successful, as has most of the Shi'ite community, in retaining its Islamic identity. This largely secretive community with its gender egalitarianism is often overlooked in studies on Islam in America. Much of the success of this community is due, however, to the fact of its centralized government. The office of Imam passes from the Imam to his descendant by designation, and the community does not participate in this process.

Daudi (Dawoodi) Bohra Isma'ilis

One late arriving immigrant Isma'ili community from India is the Daudi Bohra. They emerged from the Musta'il branch of Isma'ilism.[12] This community of "indigenous converts" is guided by ninety-three-year-old Dr. Syedna Mohammed Burhanuddin from Mumbai (formerly Bombay), India. The community is highly conservative, adhering to orthodox Shi'ite Muslim religious practices but also eagerly adopting many progressive aspects of modern culture. This propensity toward adopting technology and their stress on gender equality, with the exception of the demand that women wear the *burqa* without the face veil, are hallmarks for this old community.

The Bohra, who are primarily of Gujarati descent, live in 470 communities around the world, with almost two-thirds residing inside India. They began arriving in the United States in the 1950s and number around seven thousand. Their existence has been shrouded in mystery, as no researcher had been able to obtain access to study until Professor Jonah Blank's investigation of them in *Mullah's on the Mainframe*, published in 2001.

As with other Shi'ite communities, Bohra leaders play decisive roles in identity formation and community life. The foremost leader is the *da'i al-Mutlaq*, who is given the honorary title of Syedna and is supported by a hierarchy of leaders known as the *dawat*. All members of this community carry identity cards and are distinguished by their compliance to the dictates of the Syedna. This Syedna has further set apart his community by their emphasis on religious peace in the world. As this community begins to make its presence known in America, I am sure researchers will look more closely at it.

Differences in aspects of religious understandings between Shiʿite and Sunni Muslims are not the only differences that separate South Asian Muslims. There are within the Sunni community differences of religious ideology.

One reason for disputations in philosophy in this ethnic community where one expects "just an Islamic position" lies notably not only in the fact that there are a plurality of Islamic positions, but also in issues of class and family determining the Islamic response, which we will address later. On the Indian subcontinent and subsequently in Pakistan, there are several outstanding communities of philosophical and religious thought that emerged in resistance to British colonialism/neocolonialism and Hindu nationalism and that form the internal policies and the politics of communities in the United States.

In northern India, Deobandi sentiments reign. The founders of the Deobandi movement were reformed Sufis as well as scholars of Islam. Deobandi reemphasize what had become traditional standards of Muslim conduct using the Hanafi School of jurisprudence. Scholars have asserted that Deobandi use the Hanafi interpretations of Islamic law as a "bulwark against non-Islamic influences."[13] Their emphasis is on "Islamic knowledge" while using British institutions as the model for organization. The language of importance is Urdu. Another religious/philosophical position is that of the Tablighi Jamaʿat. The Tablighi Jamaʿat originally sought to teach Islam to those who were only marginally Muslim—those in regions where Islam had not fully penetrated and those who under British rule had strayed away from Islamic practice. Later, the Jamaʿat extended its job to include the West and those new to Islam.

The Tablighi Jamaʿat assisted in muting the callousness of the end of British rule; they emphasized discipline, mutual service, and congregational worship, prescribed study and shared activity. This was sure to bring Muslims back to Islam and out of malaise. Still another response to colonialism is found in the Barelwis's defense of the local shrines and cults of personality that had developed during Mogul reign and continued under the British. (The Barelwis are supporters of Sufism [folk tradition] and the legitimacy of Shaikhs and strines.) The *pirs* (saints) provide intercession between the worshipper and God. Most of those who take this stance see the Sufis as the only solution to religious strife, since they focus on inner spirituality, and these ideas are found in American communities also. Lastly, Jamaʿat Islami or the Islamic Party, founded by Maududi in 1941 asserted that Islam was both religion and an ideology with an activist stance and a complete legal system, which guided all aspects of life. It positioned itself against Sufism and was politically assertive in moving to put "good" Muslims into offices of social and political leadership. These stances form some of the basis of current Islamic thought in South Asia. Despite these differences, South Asian Muslims share much with South Asian Hindus regarding culture.

The Hindu Origins of Family Values

The Upanishads are the final portion of the Vedas, the primary Hindu scriptures. Traditionally, Hindus have thought of the Vedas as the work of enlightened sages who grasped the truth of how reality is composed. Most scholars attribute this foundational layer of Indian culture to the heritage of the people (Aryans) who began to infiltrate South Asia from the northwest early in the second millennium B.C.E. "The Self came from the nothingness of death and hunger, as the fruit of a desire for a positive identity."[14] But the self was alone, facing nothing, having nothing over against which to define it or with which to share.

> First, the motive for the action that produced woman and sexuality was to gain joy. Second, the Self swelled to the size and form of a present-day human couple embracing (sexually). Then it split into two. The closeness of the two parts that had been united was that of marital partners—people oriented to one another for a common being, life, and fertility.[15]

> . . . the dominance of the male voice throughout the Vedas is clear. In our text it determines that the woman should be considered the supplement of the man. He is the one suffering want and she is the one who fulfills it. So, she appears to serve his needs, while he appears as humanity in its first instance—the one whose needs determine things.[16]

In South Asian interpreted thought (Indian, Pakistani, Kashmiri, and Bangladeshi Muslim thought), the Bhagavad-Gita is possibly the most famous Hindu scripture. It presents the teachings of the god Krishna to a troubled warrior, Arjuna. The issue here is between Arjuna's position in the warrior caste and the fact that he must fight his own kin. For Arjuna "the family traditions are the basic defense against social chaos."[17] This is at the heart of South Asian culture regardless of the particularities of religion or region. Tradition is passed down as wisdom, and its absence is chaos. The coming of Islam did not change this position even though the Qur'an is clear on the possibility of the need to break with one's kin and tradition to seek the truth. South Asian culture has maintained that "if women stepped outside their accustomed roles, then children and family life would run amok,"[18] and thus fall into chaos.

The lines of descent are of ultimate importance, resulting in the need for arranged marriages to particular people with particular professions.

> The judgment that women always needed male control is much less obvious, but it is deeply rooted in Indian history. . . . women were considered more physical and less spiritual than men. They were thought to be ruled by emotion rather than reason. Women worked very hard, both at home and in agriculture or business, but their first responsibility was to produce offspring to continue the family line.[19]

So old is this thought, so embedded in the very soil that is South Asia, that even the power of the Qur'an has not loosened its control until very recently and only in a very limited way. In South Asian culture, women's obligations to men are more in number and complexity than men's obligations to women, notwithstanding the fact that men are supposed to provide everything. Women are to venerate their husbands regardless of how their husbands behave.

> The husband is supposed to provide 100 percent of everything, and there are enough dowries given so that their daughter will be treated well. They keep saying that it is the guy's responsibility. You still hear sermons at the *masjid* about this. So there is a lot of pressure on the husband who everyone goaded to get married in the first place. If a girl has been raised in a certain class then the guy needs to maintain that status, and this is justified using religion.[20]

Hindu religion and culture provides much of the basis of tradition in South Asian Muslim life, and it is what is transported as South Asian values to the United States. In the United States, however, and probably in other South Asian diasporas in the West, even though these values are under assault, they are not abandoned. While we see the tie to Hindu culture, we cannot assume there is very little that is Muslim in these lives.

5

South Asian Culture

America is recognized in many parts of the world as the land of opportunity and of great potential wealth. For most South Asian immigrants, opportunity and dreams of wealth go hand in hand with the potential to fulfill the obligations of career and family security that may not be available in the "home country."

> There is a craze to go to America. People think everything is easy here—as soon as you arrive you get a job and make lots of money. My mother always talked about getting us to America. There were lots of boys that wanted to marry me but all but one wanted to stay in India. My mom would not hear of it. She gave her consent to the one who wanted to go to America.[1]

Getting to America is still the greatest ambition of many people, especially in Pakistan where unemployment is very high and opportunity for many is almost nonexistent. This is truly a transnational community. Pakistanis have formed networks throughout the world, and travel to and from Pakistan is as frequent as it is to other parts of the family network inside the United States.

American commercials, movies, and videos all advertise the wealth of the United States and the rights of the individual to be anything s(he) wants and, as importantly, to speak freely. And these images are exported to the world. The United States is a place where "dreams can come true" overnight with or without hard labor. Imagine the effect on the rest of the world knowing that nine million Americans became millionaires from lotteries and game shows. Sixty-four people a day become millionaires in Silicon Valley alone.[2] Amazing fortunes realized overnight have caused a new mental illness—"sudden wealth syndrome," resulting in a new category of experts—"wealth counselors." The thought of all the financial possibilities that America provides is sometimes overwhelming even to Americans.

For every undereducated South Asian that makes it to American shores, there are twenty well-educated professionals or students that come with abundant academic credentials or potential, and usually some financial resources. Though this exodus of the educated is a brain drain on the subcontinent, it has not completely depleted it of its intellectuals, scientists, educators, and health professionals. The subcontinent's current population estimates are in excess of the entire United States at over a billion. Country statistics put "well-educated" at about 1 percent of the population, or approximately four to five million, and it is little more than half of that percentage that come to the United States. Other educated South Asians have either gone to other highly industrialized, technical countries such as South Africa and Australia or live in countries with large natural resources and use trading networks to build wealth. A century of British colonialism has made many well-educated Muslim South Asians averse to settling in the United Kingdom, though Britain still attracts small businessmen, writers, and laborers. The prosperity and prudent money management of these professionals in the United States has enabled them to bring over spouses and even members of the extended family. Money sent home has increased the quality of life for many family members and friends. Less fortunate South Asians, who often wind up driving cabs or working in convenience stores, have brought some notice to a community who once thrived in anonymity.

What awaits Muslim immigrants or transnationals in the United States, nonetheless, is a peculiar existence—an almost marginal existence until recently. As previously mentioned the existence is peculiar because in the American mind until recently, all Muslims are Arabs and all South Asians are "Hindoos." Now all Muslims are potential terrorists. But this is not the South Asians' only challenge. A new culture also means that none of the inherited status intact at home translates into real class status in this new country, which has its own class criteria. This is one of the forces that encourages South Asian immigrants to relentlessly pursue wealth in hopes of recapturing or raising their status along with ensuring family security. Coming from countries where the Hindu caste system has been replaced by class among Muslims, South Asian Muslims come to America in two varieties—those who were middle and upper class at home (meaning that they had inherited wealth, a profession, or worked for the government), and representatives of lower classes as relatives of professionals, and small businessmen.

Class in South Asia, as in America, also determines how business and political transactions occur. Professionals form networks of business and political relationships through reciprocities enabling "connections" when needed.

For any citizen, the political and social networks are keys to survival, learned through family connections. Immigrants have a difficult task. Initially they use what they know from "back home" only to slowly realize that they do not have the right capital for exchanges. Building trust and making the right contacts is a process in every country. It is especially tedious when there are preexisting stereotypes blocking the way.

All South Asians Are "Hindoos"—Like It or Not

In the first decade of the twentieth century,

> the so-called "Hindus" suffered from the general anti-Asian [sentiment] prevalent in the Pacific coast states at the close of the nineteenth and the beginning of the twentieth centuries. Popular magazines and leading newspapers decried the arrival of South Asians and characterized it as a "Hindu invasion" and a "tide of turbans." One journal warned its readers that the United States was about to be inundated with "Hindus" because the Vedas, scriptures of Hinduism, enjoins them to "cover the earth."[3]

Our caricatures of "Hindoos" today come from our plentiful but not diverse pictures of India through documentaries and a few movies, which are full of every orientalist imagining. India is the "incredible" but very dirty Ganges River; it is poverty; it is millions and millions of exotically beautiful people who wear "beautiful wraps" and strange but colorful turbans. India is dirty and emaciated, with poor South Asians who can barely breathe in the dirty brown air full of pollutants. Large numbers of South Asians, according to the National Geographic and Discovery Channel documentaries, are snake charmers. These enduring images, conjured up whenever India is mentioned, at the same time present a people who are a threat only to themselves as they multiply at an astonishing rate. Today, the video streams contain visions of anti-American demonstrations with pictures of the same areas of poverty. Now mobs of angry, dirty people carry signs denouncing America and burning her flag.

The picture of South Asia's unrelenting poverty and seemingly persistent chaos deters any thoughts in American minds of technological development or modernity. Speaking generally, state divisions and religious differences among South Asians are still largely invisible to the American gaze. Pakistanis look like Indians, who look like Kashmiris, who look like Bangladeshis. Muslim, Hindu, Sikh, Jain, or Christian—they are all "Hindoos." This picture of South Asians—all of them—is so firmly implanted in our minds, that in 2000 when our neoscholars/journalists attempted to stir up anger against South Asian immigrants over their former homelands' possession of nuclear arms, there initially was no response from the American public. When a response finally was evoked, it was one of fear and confusion along the lines of "What would these people know to do with nuclear arms?"

The American Muslim immigrant is currently in an "in-between place"—as Homi Bhabha describes, an "interstice—the overlap and displacement of domains of difference—that the intersubjective and collective experiences of nationness, community interest, of cultural value are negotiated," and "these in-between spaces provide the terrain for elaborating strategies of selfhood—

singular or communal. . . . "[4] This description is very important in the explanation of culture attempted in this text.

Bhabha, in heavily nuanced and complicated language, describes a very critical component of most immigrants' existence. There is always an ambivalence at the site of colonial dominance—the anxiety over which way to go. Do colonizers win because we are weak or do they win because they are right? Those who dominate and force the oppressed into patterns of behavior shaped by their definition of what it is to be human often then decry that very behavior. The questions posed by the colonized become: How could we show our ability to achieve and succeed by their standards, thus proving our worth and conversely distinguishing ourselves from the truly unable? How can we prove that we are not a part of those homogenous descriptions of the third world?

Perhaps descriptions of the postcolonial psyche by scholars such as Bhabha in his attempt to describe the internal struggle, the resistances, and the spaces in which both occur are just too new for many of us to begin to understand. The presence of Muslim immigrants from all over the world in America provides an excellent field for study of the reactions of immigrants from various classes and ethnicities that meet and have to live in the same public space. Their colonizations differ only in degree and place. Their need to be free of the chaos is as common a thread as their desire to contribute positively to the future of America. One problem for all immigrants and their hosts is identity. As with most people, the immigrant is proud to be a new citizen in the United States. Does leaving the root culture mean that one gives up that identity totally, or can the new and old live together?

Transnational American Muslims of South Asian origins are in such a "moment of transit." They are no longer completely South Asian to either their ethnic or adopted cultures. In the ethnic culture they look like the majority but think and act differently in observable ways. This state of affairs is not new as in every culture where they have migrated they exist in the same configuration. In the United States, almost irrespective of the length of time in residence, they think and act on intimate terms with the history and current affairs of "back home." Many transnational South Asian Muslims are a blend of Hindu cultural artifacts, Islamic knowledge, and British etiquette with American tastes. Others have become hyper-Americanized with little association with anything except the most extreme of American tastes. In between these extremes lie those who are clinging to a notion of remaining who they are while living in America.

Some researchers on immigrant communities seem to take Sanford Ungar's position in *Fresh Blood*.

> Most of these new immigrants, of course, like those who came before them, are self-selected. Legal or not, they tend to be the adventurers, the

> risk-takers, the strong of mind and body who can cope with being uprooted and landing in a totally new environment.[5]

Other scholars, such as demographer Leon F. Bouvier, writing in *Peaceful Invasion: Immigration and Changing America* assert " . . . new immigrants will fail to adapt and will be swept up in 'cultural separatism.'"[6] Of course elements of both statements are true even though they almost totally contradict each other and leave out the particularities of the worldviews of the immigrants, and presume some embedded representations of immigrants to be true. Bouvier and others focus totally on the need of first-generation immigrants to maintain the "home" culture and language as if they exclude the reality of their present space. Transnationals maintain the home culture and language because they use the language in their networks and travel home frequently. While this is a primary need of all immigrants, it also obviates the particularities of the host culture and its general attitudes toward specific immigrant communities. Ungar and others mask the dislocation of immigrants as if the move to a totally new culture is similar to moving from one house to another in the same city or another part of the same country. In a global economy, where an immigrant community networks with a same-language community elsewhere, language maintenance is a must just as it is for family relations.

In a very general overview of South Asian culture as it is in the United States, we witness obsessions with class, color, profession; a general subordination of women; a British understanding of etiquette and status; and issues of identity.

Settling in America

The first impression and reaction of arriving immigrants to the United States varies with the individual, of course, but most approach their new home with a positive attitude.

> My initial reactions getting off the plane was that everything was so different. I spoke English, but with an accent that was different. The people dressed differently. I was wearing a sari. There was nothing that was familiar. . . . I had never been on a plane before, I held my breath. I was fascinated by the buildings. I really liked the skyscrapers. I was amazed at how quiet the roads were. In India, all you hear are the horns of cars every few seconds.[7]

> When I was leaving home, I was very sad. Everyone was crying, especially the older people like my grandmother. They were afraid that I would not come back to visit India in their lifetime.[8]

Muslims from South Asia make up the largest ethnic group of immigrant Muslims in the United States at approximately 26.4 percent of an estimated six to nine million Muslims.[9] They live and work in small towns such as Radcliff, Kentucky, and large, metropolitan areas such as Chicago and New York. They are taxi drivers, merchants, physicians, housewives, engineers, lawyers, and teachers. They differ on just about everything including politics, how to be a Muslim minority, education, social integration and the priority of ethnic identity, and whether or not to participate in American social life. Many South Asian Muslims avoid intimate social contact with Americans, choosing to live socially mostly in an insulated world of South Asian movies, music, and languages. Others choose to be more American than most Americans. For these Muslims everything America does is fine, no matter how just or unjust.

Some are mesmerized by the technologically advanced American society and are eager to adopt everything western including the vices. Some left Islam behind when they boarded the plane to the United States, while others left it behind once they felt the freedom to not be Muslim, still others thought Islam archaic at home and rediscovered it in the United States. Still other South Asian Muslims are strongly committed to Islamic values yet do not want to be isolated, asserting the need to share Islamic values with other Americans.

Early South Asian Muslim transnationals first arrived and sought any community of Muslims. However, when a significant number of immigrants of the same philosophical position and from the same area arrived, they raised money, and moved away from the main body of Muslims into their own place as they have done around the world. It is important here to briefly recount in the American story to the subcontinent to explain these philosophies because of their hegemony over the nature of Islamic discourse and the communities' discursive practices in the United States. All of these philosophies we examined earlier are present in the United States and are in contest over who will have the greatest hegemony over the definition of Islam.

Recall the philosophical/ideological positions described in the preceding chapter—Deobandi, Barelwis, and Tablighi Jamaʿat. Muslims from the Deobandi tradition will not easily participate in gatherings that include women. In these mosques women and children are totally separated from men either in the same room behind a heavy curtain or partition or on another floor.

The influences of the United States are seen as corrupt and to be avoided at all costs. Deobandis attempt to prevent any compromise of Islamic values with the "freedoms" in everyday life. Muslims must keep *halal* (within the range of what is islamically permissible) at all costs. Associations with non-Muslims should be kept at a minimum; children must attend Islamic schools; women must obey their husbands no matter what the issue; national and local politics are to be avoided as are Muslims not living under Islamic rule. While these are outward markers, it is Deobandi thought that emerges as a real challenge. Eschewing all things western is a challenge when living in the United States.

In contrast those who are Sufi or Barelwis in upbringing or orientation are far more liberal in gender relations, permitting women to have voices in the mosque and welfare of the community. They are strong supporters of education of girls along with boys into professional life. The Tablighi Jamaʿat's philosophy falls somewhere in between the Sufis and the Deobandi as they do believe in activism in the communities in which they live; they do believe in women's activism (though in separate meetings), and in outreach to non-Muslim Americans. The reader should note however, that any South Asian Muslim may be a collage of all these stances. Many young South Asian Muslims raised in one tradition are opting to blend stances on a number of issues. Some believe in the necessity of political activism and female inclusion in community conversations for example, but have found themselves uncomfortable initially as they work and study with non-Muslim women/men in close quarters and practice gender separation at home.

Gender practices are not the only manifestation of religious philosophical stance. Participation in politics here and abroad is also indicated by philosophical stance. For example, believers in Deobandi thought are also generally supporters of Deobandi *madaaris* (pl. of *madrassah*) in Pakistan and exporters of salafism. They are more likely not to favor any U.S. intervention in Pakistan's affairs even when that intervention is sought by Pakistan's government.

A host of issues arise for non-Muslim and non–South Asian Muslims in attempting to understand the South Asian community. For the non-Muslim American media attempting to gauge the Muslim communities' thoughts on different issues, there have been instances of shock at the anti-American sentiments expressed by some communities. Lacking the knowledge of "who is who," reporters often attribute anti-American sentiments to all Muslims in general, further alienating other Muslims who are just as shocked at those anti-American responses. Yet despite the diversity of this community, there are basic commonalities and one is the family.

The Family

Most South Asians acknowledge that their community is one that has a predominance of two occupations: doctors and engineers. It is not just that the community has a predominance of these professionals but also that material success is important to family status and survival inside the ethnic community.

Family integrity, longevity, and cohesiveness are central, and some would say critical, to existence in South Asia. The fact that family *is* the community is important in this study. Americans also hold the notion of family in high esteem but generally do not even come close to the notion of family as community. In South Asia the family controls its members desires and pursuits. Community in the United States is experienced on a number of levels—blood-related family, neighborhood and work friends. Intimate relationships are formed in each of these spaces, sometimes even with the loyalty of blood kinship or in lieu of it.

Parents rear children with both love and firmness, binding them in loyalty to the family, and the family all over the world is the community. All adults in the family along with the society affirm the child-rearing pattern, as do film and music. One goal of the family is social acceptability.

> It's the idea of pleasing people. It's not just a women's thing. It's a culture that doesn't stand up to any conflict in many different things. Even when you talk to people here having a horrible time at work, you would say, "you should talk to your boss about that." They do not want to stand up. Some of it is not standing up to authority in general but some of it is a culture that wants to cater, to look after, sometimes at the expense of themselves—most of the times themselves.[10]

In several conversations with Muslims from South Asia, this sentiment was persistently repeated. It should be noted here that youth is speaking. Many of the young people interviewed for this text have spent most of their lives here in the United States, though with frequent travel back to South Asia and other places where family lives. Yet they manifest the western notion of learning to protest any infraction of what is perceived as a right. Their parents, however, usually experienced the aftermath of British colonialism/neocolonialism, which demanded acquiescence to injustice and sometimes brutally suppressed groups who challenged the status quo. This one generational cultural difference provides the substance of a lot of frustration.[11]

South Asians are known to be hard workers and loyal to the institutions, firms, and/or businesses for which they work, although in the United States they have found that loyalty no longer translates into job security. Professions are taken with extreme seriousness and there is generally an absence of second careers. Employment politics on the whole are avoided to keep good relationships all around because it is work that comes first. It is very important for the South Asian Muslim to have a good reputation, to keep on top of tasks, and to have excellent evaluations as these are the stairs to recognition, promotions, and prestige in the Muslim community and certainly in the family. Also,

> You just never say no to a guest. They (folks from South Asia) are very proud of that and they uphold those values. The formality of a situation is just more important than convenience.[12]

In the West, where ruthlessness, haste, impatience, and rudeness are increasingly perceived as the qualities of the powerful and, therefore, a successful person, South Asian courtesy, patience, and politeness are often interpreted as the signs of backwardness. South Asian Muslims are far from weak and certainly do not lack ambitions though many of them lack the obvious aggressiveness of the West, even when they have lived here for decades. Women strive not only to please husbands and children, they strive to represent their families as enclaves of serenity and happiness—first to their extended families, and to the community and the society at large. Both men and women joyfully sacrifice for the betterment of their children thus insuring some measure of security for themselves in sickness and old age and insuring self-satisfaction, though children sometimes complain of no opportunity to pursue their own dreams. Adult children take great pride in what they can do for their parents, much like American children but even more so as they are in competition with their ethnic peers to make sure parents are secure. This very effective method of family security and support in South Asian communities usually works well to safeguard the elderly from isolation and potential poverty.

The pervasive focus on social acceptability, family cohesiveness, and security has produced a community where children are reared to excel, be mindful of their parents' desires, and to struggle for the best at every level. When this does not happen, the shame on the family is made even more intense by the South Asian community as the gossip begins. Happiness is every child married and doing well, demonstrable "good living," and the parent's relative assurance of their security in old age. Thus parents begin early in their search for suitable (class, status, profession) mates for their children. This is done by getting to know families and most recently in marriage forums in large ethnic conferences and conventions.

> Marriage is a major concern. A young woman must be married right out of college if not before. Women delay going for a second degree because it is understood that you don't want to be considered too educated.[13]

The priority placed on marriage however, has other advantages—it diminishes the opportunity for situations prevalent in American society such as promiscuity, premarital and extramarital sex, and out-of-wedlock births. This is not to say that such situations are not present in these Muslim families, but the incidence is a tiny fraction of what occurs in general American society. Young women and men are taught loyalty to the family from childhood. Women are taught traditional homemaking values no matter what their geographical location, profession, or status. Media and other family members from the home country are used to further affirm lifestyle patterns. Hindi movies and their reigning artists are imported to the United States by the planeload.

In their affirmation of culture, many of these films focus on what is normal and abnormal, especially with respect to marriage. Daughters are primed for arranged marriages through the movies, friends, and families. South Asian movies have been used to define culture for second and third generations who have never even been to India or Pakistan.

> We were not allowed to watch any English movies growing up because that was all promiscuous. But we were allowed to watch South Asian movies, which were very promiscuous too. That [movies] was where you saw the arrangement of marriage and if you have been watching since you were six years old that's your concept of marriage. I thought that these people were going to come over, because this is the scenario: you bring tea into the living room and they show how the girl is really nervous and dropping tea on the floor. She walks in like a goddess, everybody stands up. Her eyes are facing the floor.[14]

> In films, and TV old spinsters simply do not exist, all women get married if they live long enough. In novels, commercial films, and TV plays, women are self-depreciating mothers who sacrifice themselves for the sake of their children. In movies and legends only long-suffering women are ever rewarded with respect.[15]

Despite living in the West, cultural traditions reign.

> My marriage was arranged by my mother. I went back to India to get married. I was given the final say. I had confidence in arranged marriages because my mom had more experience and knowledge and also because that was the custom in India.[16]

Marriage is the occupation of choice as it confers status on the family and serves as the beginning of the preparations for that social security system.

> Women are looked at pretty much to serve men—starting from being obedient daughters to dutiful sisters, to great wives and great moms. You are going to go to the best schools and get the best education but your ultimate goal is to be married to a particular person with a certain career. The talk about career and what you are going to do with the education kind of stops at marriage.[17]

The extent to which parents are able to impose their will on their children and that they are backed by a community may be what is different from what happens in the United States and other western countries. Independence in social life and family relations is severely discouraged.

> I feel Indians, overall, especially the middle- to upper-class people, are very class and profession oriented. They really want to maintain the culture by marrying into the same kind of status. They feel that the only way they can provide stability for their daughters is to marry them to stable men as opposed to them having their own independence—like doctors and engineers and computer scientists or businessmen who are working for a top firm, not entrepreneurs. I mean, very seldom do you hear, "Oh, my daughter's marrying someone who is starting up his own business." Usually it's people who are MBAs. When people found out that I was going to marry a journalist, they said, "And what else does he do." Of course when he became a lawyer, everyone said, "Oh you did very well."[18]

While part of maintaining culture is found in keeping the right status, social class and color are high priorities. While Muslims in South Asia abhor the Hindu caste system, they have held tightly to this system by converting it into their practice of a system of social class and color.

> We're very, very color conscious and I'm not talking about three generations ago but I am talking about my friends who have children and who are listening to their mothers to eat certain foods so that their babies will be lighter colored. Women are very excited to marry their sons to women from cultures where they're light skinned. Not necessarily that they are non-Muslim but, you know, that they take pride in lighter colored children. Here even, folks say, "I saw the cutest baby, he was so fair." They're conscious. You see young women with beautiful black hair; they have totally highlighted it so that it is blond. There is the need to be light and a need to be skinny.
>
> If you look at the Indian movies for example and you listen to the songs. There is a lot of reference to frail, light-skinned women. Delicate, frail, thin, long, those are all parts of songs—*nazook*. When you look at Indian movies, everybody is dancing around, and a guy is singing to a girl—he is saying "this is a season for people who are light skinned or why are you worried you have such fair skin." They use the word *gori,* which means you are fair. So a lot of it is part of the Indian movies and stuff. People have been extremely upset when their sons have decided to marry some-

> one who was really dark skinned, even if the person was Indian. This is a really big issue.
>
> There are commercials in India for skin lighteners. The most famous commercial is by Nexus. Somebody bought it for me when I was seventeen or eighteen years old because they said it would make me lighter; I broke out in zits (lots of laughter). The name of the cream is *Fair and Lovely.* The commercial is this guy and his family are looking for a girl and go to another family's house and they see this girl there and they say she is very nice but she is very *saunli.* This means that she is a shade of brown. That's their big concern. Well the girl's family notices that. One of her friends tells her that she needs to use this cream. So when they come the next time they are so in love with her because she looks so white. So the marriage takes place. You can buy these products in South Asian stores here too. To have someone say that you look good, you are so fair is taken as a compliment. When I was a kid I was told not to drink a lot of tea because it would make me darker.
>
> Even when I was younger, babies looked cute if they were white and chubby. I had to live on my own, work with a lot of different people to get over it—to see beauty in people. It is hard for people from South Asia to make friends with people who are dark. People seek to have more white friends.[19]

The shock of these statements from young and old women from South Asia is only balanced when one realizes that though they are color conscious in the extreme, they know it is wrong. Young men and women readily admit the extreme color consciousness while their parents patently deny its existence with the same amount of passion. Though the younger adults express discomfort with their color consciousness, they have not been able to make it a topic for community conversation, their openness, however, is certainly one of the challenges to the hegemony of their parents.

More Challenges

While many young women are driven by community standards to the border of anorexia, use whitening creams, understand marriage as an essential part of their being human, and honor their husbands in all things, they are not all oppressed nor do they all live without deep feelings about a culture that gives them little control over their lives. They value the cohesiveness of family and its integrity. They want their daughters married to men who are stable and who can give the same kind of care that the parents have given. It is important to know that the assets that took a whole lifetime to earn will be used well. In exchange, they give up some of what Western women see as "freedom." Males are still raised to pursue the highest professions, spend their wealth on family, and strive for recognition and are beginning to protest.

> I was raised on stories of how I must become a doctor or engineer. I must study all the time and not even rest for a minute. Everything in my life—status, ability to marry a fair woman depended on my study. I must become wealthy and not get into looking at music, art or anything that was not a doctor or engineer. I must improve the status of the family. Nobody ever asked if I was a good person or if I was ethical. Just make money as a doctor or engineer.[20]

> I was a premed student for one year. It wasn't me. I wanted something different. My parents yelled, threatened to cut me off from everything. I went ahead and majored in business and since then they have criticized everything I do. I am the black sheep of the family. This is hard because they loved me when they thought I was going to be a doctor like my father.

> Young men too have pressures to measure up to family expectations. The community who will either ridicule or think less of the family whose boys are not in medicine or the natural sciences reinforces "measuring up."[21]

Most of the young men I spoke with, even those who were pursuing elite careers, expressed the discomfort of being forced into professions whether or not they were able to succeed or even liked it. They wanted to have the freedom to choose but did not want to "fail the family" or "make my mother cry." They saw themselves torn between what they had known all their lives and the endless possibilities in American culture. They were moving slowly away from what they saw as cultural limitations.

As a matter of fact, most of the young men that I spoke with refused to acknowledge their ethnic heritage and preferred to be just "American Muslims" rather than Pakistani or Indian. Many of them had never been to the homelands of their parents except for very short visits, did not like it much, felt foreign (even if they had been forced into marriages with girls from home), and wanted to rid themselves of cultural expressions of Islam. The first American generation seems to be caught between worlds. They are in resistance to any attempt to simply rely on the cultural knowledge of their parents, though they are very much still traditional. One young man put it simply:

> I have friends from just about every ethnicity and I like it that way. I don't want to just have friends from "home." My parents consider this bad. But I really don't care. I don't bring my friends home because they would not be welcome and this makes me feel bad but I will move out as soon as school is over and then I can have my friends over to visit me when I want. Who wants to play basketball or workout with South Asians? I know that I will still marry the girl my parents like but I won't be happy.[22]

Whether or not being different from parents will result in a wider acceptance of people of all classes and colors is yet to be seen, but some young people are determined. Nevertheless, these well-educated young adults, along with their parents, deprive South Asia of needed leadership in Islam and in global systems. This has been seen almost everywhere since September 11, 2001. In the first months after September 11, young American Muslims were desperate to have a say about Islam and Muslims. A few radio talk shows asked their opinions, and the listeners heard very articulate renderings on the subject of terrorism and the Muslim world. However, after three years of listening to the media and the government bash Islam and Muslims and witnessing the profiling and detentions of their family members and friends, some of their rhetoric is changing.

They have found that being born in America is not enough to make them citizens. They are in a special category—limbo. At any time to prove that the government is right in its war against Islam, they too can be detained without reason or rights because of the country of origin of their parents.

The second American generation is breaking other rules.

> The crowd thickens on the small dance floor at S.O.B.'s, a world music club and the venue of Bhangra Basement, the first regular *bhangra* night at a mainstream club in New York, hosted by the ubiquitous DJ Rekha. The insistent beat of the *dhol*, the percussion base of the traditional North Indian folk dance known as *bhangra* in Punjab, pounds out over the techno and reggae tracks reverberating amidst the tightly packed bodies.[23]

> Indian American subculture has become a new site for the collision of identity politics and the marketing of ethnic styles. A second generation Indian American subculture that revolves around the use of two commodities, music and fashion.[24]

Bhangra crosses ethnic, socioeconomic, and religious lines. The study cited here focused on the "question of negotiating identities." Naming this subculture "remix youth culture," Maira discovered the ambiguities in the lives of these young people.

> . . . revealing source of tension within this Indian (Indian, Pakistani, Bangladeshi) American world of dance parties and social gatherings is the contestation of heterosexual and gender roles and of racial identifications performed in these spaces. Many informants spoke of the perception among their peers that for women, beauty was inextricably associated with fair skin, the "long black hair-type thing" that mirrors the alluring image of Indian film actresses—icons familiar to many in the second generation—and, often, a thin body, in keeping with dominant ideals pervading fashion and media.[25]
>
> Many note that a "hoody," or streetwise hip-hop, image is not considered as appealing for women in this subculture as it is for men, and the pervasive image of desirable femininity rests on less androgynous-looking, designer-inspired New York fashion. Provocative clothing styles are often popular for women at Indian parties; tight-fitting club wear, in its latest incarnation of slinky hip-hugging pants, halter tops, and miniskirts is often worn to allow a flash or more of leg or midriff. Some sport a diamond nose stud or nose ring in a nod to ethnic style. More common is a cosmeticized appearance—black rimmed eyes, dark lipstick, and arched eyebrows—and an emphasis on slimness, if not thinness. Several men acknowledged the pervasiveness of the heterosexual double standard for Indian American women, a standard that allows for a seductive, party-going girlfriend but expects a wife to uphold the sanctity of family and, by extension, tradition. The dichotomy of "Indian" versus "American" thus becomes a gendered and sexualized contrast.[26]

Transnationals fight for the maintenance of ethnic identity and tradition and often lament the decision to come to America.

Families cope with the habits of traditional cultures and the opportunities of the global village. Traditional cultures have built-in stress producers and reducers. Stress is a common component in immigrant marital life whether or not the extended family is present, though the extended family does indeed relieve mothers. Many of the South Asian female immigrants were used to households with servants and/or large extended families "back home." Immigration itself has put marriages under a new stress—violation of tradition.

One cornerstone of South Asian life is the arranged marriage. At "home" prospective grooms can be scrutinized by the prospective bride's family members before any engagement takes place. Now there is the groom who lives in the West who can say anything about what he does and how much money he makes. Young men with fifteen thousand American dollars to spend on presents for the family of the intended bride seem to be telling the truth when they assert that they are indeed wealthy in America and ready for marriage. They can even claim class status through the appearance of wealth.

One short story especially makes this duplicity clear. Chitra Banerjee Divakaruni, a Hindu author, offers in her text, *Arranged Marriage*, the tale, "Silver Pavements, Golden Roofs," the story of a beginning graduate student who comes to stay with her aunt in Chicago. The man her aunt married presented himself to the family "back home" as a successful "owner of an automobile empire in America." When the niece arrives in Chicago she finds that "the man runs only a small auto-repair garage and the couple live in a dingy apartment in an undesirable part of the city." The aunt could not return home in shame. Nevertheless, the arranged marriage is still tradition and expected.

Arranged marriages, the talk of many feminists in the West as one firm example of the oppression of South Asian women irrespective of their religion can be viewed from another perspective. Gender separation is the ideal in Muslim cultures. The reality is that young men and women do in fact see each other.

This process, described in great detail in other places in this text, lends itself to marital strife. In many of the home cultures, women worked in the home or, in limited ways, in gender-segregated spaces at home. In downtown Lahore, one does not find female waitresses, for example. Here in the United States, there are several scenarios. For those in the middle class income and status are often augmented by two paychecks, and there is often an absence of extended family to assist with chores and baby-sitting. Professional South Asian women often find themselves working closely with men. For some this is a volatile situation in that the woman must be vigilant about a professional attitude along with keeping herself above reproach in situations when she may be alone with a male. She must also assure her husband of her conduct.

A significant number of nonprofessional women who come with professional husbands were used to servants at home and find themselves in the awkward situation of learning how to cook, clean, and mind their own children, all at the same time. Overwhelmed by these tasks, they begin to demand that their husbands either find them some help from home, as they need to be able to communicate the specifics of their needs, or that their husbands take over some of the tasks. Still other women find themselves working long, hard hours in their husband's business. Entrepreneurial opportunities such as Seven-Eleven, White Hen, or gas station ownership are generally successful only with the assistance of nonpaid help such as wives. Many of these women are forced to discard their demure upbringing in order to face the rush of demands from people of all ethnicities and both genders. They are often forced to keep their anxieties hidden because the business is their only income.

Husbands, on the other hand, as with the women who work, are often overwhelmed by the demands of the American workplace. How one works, punctuality, orderliness, loyalty, and grueling hours are mainstays of the American workplace, taking tolls on everyone's relationship but particularly those coming from regions where the pace of living is much slower. One young Pakistani man who worked for a large technology firm requested a short leave to go home and get married. His employer, a large international technology conglomerate, assumed that this was to be taken out of his vacation time and gave him a two-week leave. This did not translate culturally, and this young man stayed for two months. He was outraged when he came back to work and found that he no longer had a job or a sponsor. Others have found that work does not include the performance of religious worship. Separation of church and state is one of the values that make America attractive. Muslim insistence on prayer time is often viewed as "beginning down a path that will destroy America" because it is putting religion in the work place. Times have changed since September 11, 2001, and members of all the Abrahamic faiths are bringing religion to work.

Another work situation that deserves special attention here in this community is that of the professional who is "licensed back home" but not in the United States. Many professionals such as pharmacists, physicians, and lawyers must pass board examinations or take additional classes in the United States to practice. In the interim they have to support themselves and their families. It is not unusual to find trained professionals driving cabs or working at the Seven-Eleven. As anyone could imagine, the frustration level is extraordinarily high. All of these things contribute to marital strife. The demands of work, care of children, and housework are having much the same effect on many American households. What differs somewhat is knowledge of available resources to assist in coping with marital discord.

The South Asian family generally feels that these intimate concerns cannot be discussed outside of the husband and wife. In-laws, if told of problems, do not usually sympathize with the problems, and their advice is generally to tell couples to ignore the problem and it will go away. There is nowhere to go inside of the community because gossip is one thing to be avoided and the community is very "nosy." Many women find that they have no recourse but to wait until things get better. It is also a fact that in this community, once a female divorces she is no longer eligible for marriage inside the community unless she is extraordinarily wealthy or has very high status. As one interviewee puts it:

> No matter if a woman is raped, no man wants a woman who has been had by other men. She might as well become a professional or a scholar if she gets divorced because no Indian or Pakistani man will have her unless she becomes someone with an extremely high status job. If men get divorced

there is no stigma, if men decided they want a girlfriend on the side, it's all right, they are men and can do no wrong.[27]

Nevertheless some women from South Asia are deciding that it is better to live without abuse and take the communal gossip than to live in fear. In some cases their families assist them, but rarely. Most of these women never return to any activity in the community because of the gossip and stares. Again, the second and third generations and the courageous among the first generation are making strides in this area with some male support. Increasingly South Asian men are speaking out against the abuses by their brothers and fathers, and encouraging the use of professional marriage counselors.

The cultural norms remain as do the challenges. Change, however, is on the horizon as the young, educated South Asians, male and female, know America as their home. They are seeking ways to fit in without losing their religious heritage and the values it gives.

6

Islam and the Arabs

The Making of an Image

One image of Arabs and Islam that emerges says: all Arabs are threatening and the evil other; all Arabs are Muslim; thus, all Muslims are evil, threatening, and other. Our investigation, however, must take two paths almost simultaneously. The other or mirror image, always present as a veiled shadow, is that of the Arab Muslim woman—equally mysterious, oppressed, and other. This inquiry examines some of the modes of discourse by which this image became a part of the American conscience. Toward that end we will briefly examine scholarship and media. In the category of scholarship, we will again explore theology, history, and anthropology. In the area of media, we will investigate some of the views of film, documentary, broadcast, and print vehicles that have contributed to these images. Theology is our starting point because it provides much of the legitimacy for a specific Christian view of a Muslim "other" that becomes an American view, which would likely have reached Christian congregations in sermons or classes over the centuries.

Islam and Christianity

Islam met Christianity at its birth in the Arabian Peninsula. From the beginning of this relationship, hostilities have been at the core of all conversations.

> The essential differences that separate Christianity and Islam are about Revelation. For Christians the prophetic preparation of the Jews leads to a single event, the Incarnation, which is the inauguration of the Messianic Kingdom; for Catholics this Kingdom is the sacramental life of the Church. For Muslims, too, there is just one Revelation, of the only religion, Islam. Or submission to God; but it was made again and again through successive prophets.
>
> The integrity of the Scriptures became a key issue with Christian polemicists, but as they resented the doctrines of Islam, and saw them in the light of their own preconceptions, they inevitably deformed them.[1]

Yes, the assertions of Islam regarding monotheism challenge the Trinitarian view, however it is explained, that sits at the heart of Christian belief and thought. Due to this difference, Christian theologians have preserved a directed negative discourse on Muhammad (pbuh) and the fundamental Islamic belief that Jesus was a prophet, not God.

Christian reactions to Islam are documented from an early date. A formula for its abjuration for converts has reasonably been thought to date from the first generations after the rise of Islam, and is related to the work of Saint John of Damascus, himself born about fifty years after the *hijra*. The formula takes an unusually severe attitude in condemning whatever a Muslim believes, including the whole of what he believes about God and about Christ, although, according to the Christian faith, some of that is true.[2]

There remain points of serious contention between Islam and Christianity that revolve around issues such as the Trinity, the conception of sin, and the details of worship in the twenty-first century. To the Muslim, the miraculous birth of Jesus and the virginity of Mary are part of faith—God said, 'be' and Jesus became. To the Christian the miracle is not only of the birth, but also the descent of God into man. In Islam there is no original sin (a moral blight on the soul that humans are born with) because the original couple was created innocent and can choose to be obedient or disobedient and forgiven when they are disobedient if their behavior changes. In Islam humans are born in "primordial innocence and are judged by their merits." Just these two issues alone make for tense interreligious dialogue when there is any dialogue.

These issues however, are important for more than theological discussions. These different understandings of God's relationship to man have formed Christianity and Islam differently. Regardless, it is the differences that inform our contemporary understanding that Islam is heretical—a distortion of Christianity, or a "failed" Christianity. Historical accounts of Christian encounters with Islam and Muslims further cement these theological polemics as "common" knowledge.

History, Anthropology and Islam

Every culture has its historians and places its own community at the center of history. While most of us are taught that history is a chronological review of the facts, in fact, history is a reconstruction of those facts from the historian's vantage point, and communities tell their histories from a vantage point that places their world at the center.[3] But, ironically, for our purposes we have to explore European history and its uniqueness in order to explain the renditions of Islamic history that are typically available to the American reader. It is understood that European history would begin with Europeans. What is different, however, is that European history positions itself as the locus of all other histories—especially that of Islam.

> We know how the traditional story runs; history began in the "East"—in Mesopotamia and Egypt (but not paradise, still further east, as the medieval Westerners had said); the torch was then passed successively to Greece and Rome and finally to the Christians of northwestern Europe, where medieval and modern life developed. During the Middle Ages, Islam temporarily was permitted to hold the torch of science, which properly belonged to the West, until the West was ready to take it over and carry it forward. India, China, and Japan also had ancient civilizations but were isolated from the mainstream of history and "contributed" still less to it (that is to Western Europe). In modern times Western Europe expanded over the rest of the world, so that Islam and India and China have ceased to be isolated, and have entered the orbit of the ongoing Western civilization, now becoming a world civilization.[4]

European historians and cartographers succeeded in making Europe both a continent and the center of the world. The history of the rest of the world, in one way or another, became subordinate to the history of Europe. With "the West" (now including the United States) as the locus of industrialization, modernization, and technology, the historical achievements of the rest of the world are again isolated. It is where *Western* scholars focus their sight that is important. Regarding Islam, the eye settled on the Mediterranean and that section of northern Africa that has been dubbed "the Middle East." The focus on the Mediterranean is interesting because there is a Mediterranean culture of family loyalty, honor, and shame that Muslims share with the Greeks, Italians, Portuguese, and others—forming a Mediterranean family, so to speak.

Mediterranean Muslims, however, are separated from a primary part of their heritage according to modern Western history and are isolated. With a focus primarily on the Arab cultures of the Mediterranean and the Middle East, Islam becomes synonymous with Arab, and Arab with Muslim. As stated previously, all Arabs are threatening, and evil others, all Arabs are Muslim; thus all Muslims are evil, threatening, and other and they all live in the Middle East, which is in the Mediterranean.

Anthropology serves to affirm these historical divisions as it examines the facets of a society as discrete units with no apparent link to a whole. This obscures most of the important meanings of cultural traditions in a region or civilizational culture, especially in the case of Islam. Anthropologists have thus provided a wealth of information on small villages and towns. Though most of this information is selected for its exotic quotient, it nevertheless is given to us as slivers of pictures of life in the world. There is just enough to amuse or spur a little interest on the part of the viewer but never enough to cause inquirers to see the people of Islam and their lives as a whole or in relationship to anything else such as surrounding peoples or even the world. When it comes to the Muslim world, in the small section of the Muslim world examined, those villages that have the most peculiar houses, or women who cover themselves in some colorful way, or men who all go to a particular café are chosen, largely in the Arab portion of the Mediterranean or the Middle East, to represent all Arabs, Islam, and all Muslims.

Since many anthropological studies of Muslim cultures are primarily on Arab populations, the conclusions of the readers of those texts—including *National Geographic*, encyclopedias, and subsequent documentaries are necessarily that all Muslims are Arabs and all Arabs are Muslim—strange and threatening. Those who live in the Arab world are also never shown in any contact with each other or other Muslims. The fact that some Arabs are Christian is rarely mentioned as if to make sure that readers understand the preferred propaganda that "all Muslims are Arabs and all Arabs are Muslim." Even the fact that Arabic speakers comprise at least twenty-two countries of many different ethnicities and nationalities is obscured.

Anthropological researches have been the primary culprits in creating the exotic. Space was created in "the lure of far-distant lands" while the dimension of time was cast in "the pursuit of the historical other."[5] By space I mean distance in terms of both geography and development. The other lives far away and thus has no contact with civilization, modernity, or technology. The exotic dimension is present in what is focused on. Exotic by definition means "foreign, strange or different in a way that is striking or fascinating." Of course the referent here is the West. Anthropologists and others have sought to examine communities that meet these criteria all over the world, and almost any Muslim community is a candidate when its self-presentation is compared with that of the West. The exotic other is now a descriptor permanently attached to both the Arab world and to Islam. One researcher, Sarah Graham-Brown asserts:

> One of the central features of this vision of the Orient, which is most evident in popular writings and visual imagery, but which also informed many works of scholarship, was the concept of a society where all aspects of life—culture, politics, economics and personal relationships—could be explained by reference to the religion of Islam. In this essentialist view, Islam offered an explanatory touchstone for the behavior of people from otherwise diverse cultures, ethnic groups and social classes.[6]

This anthropological work was at its height during the era of European colonialism and produced volumes of accounts of travel, photography, and literature on the region defined as "the Middle East" for the twentieth century.

Simultaneously, these researches and adventures propagated the notion that the backwardness, also called tradition, rested with the women. Arab Muslim women became the objects of an ambiguous gaze—veiled, oppressed, secluded, and simultaneously the centerpieces of sexual paradise as they seductively dance and flirt. Using a slight variation on our model syllogism we can say—all Arab women are Muslim, strange, veiled, oppressed, and other; all Muslim women are Arab; thus Islam veils, secludes, and oppresses Muslim women.

One of the first images, prior to our war on Afghanistan in 2001, was one of dirty, veiled, wide-eyed (to be translated as ignorant and innocent) Muslim women. They needed us to save them from their husbands, fathers, brothers, and sons. Without our help these women would continue to be unfulfilled. Just as the young boys needed to fly kites, the girls needed to go to school even though they were starving.

Photography provided anthropology with a means to appear neutral in its investigations. The invention of photography (1839) during the height of European imperialism provided anthropologists with an indispensable instrument to categorize and create images. Anthropologists did not have to say anything about these "strange" people they encountered; their photographs of veiled Muslim women, sometimes posed sexually, other times clustered together with forlorn expressions, did the speaking. Bruce Lawrence summarizes:

> Behind the hostile Muslim men, Americans imagine the faces of Muslim women, homebound creatures marked alike by seclusion from the outside world and apparent oppression by their tyrannical husbands (and their religion)[parenthesis mine].[7]

The unnamed conclusion aimed for by the syllogism is that Islam comprises Middle Eastern societies, all of which are the same and this is because Islam is monolithic. Additionally, Americans were compelled into patriotism.

The role media play as primary disseminators of the facts is critical to our enterprise, as we saw earlier in this text.

> In view of the serious concerns of the nation at war [during the Gulf War], the authorities debate whether or not the Super Bowl (January 1991) should be cancelled, but decided finally that it would be good for the morale of the men and women at war, as well as for those at home, to go forward with it. Viewers who tuned in were caught up in the drama of a hallowed sports saga amid the anxiety and suspense of a nation at war. In a spectacular way the televised coverage fused a combination of loyal-

ties—the nation's war effort in the Middle East, to the favorite teams, and to the American way of life.

Patriotism was the major motif of the game. The opening ceremonies were military extravaganzas that featured representatives from the armed services; cameras moved in with tight shots of their stalwart faces and the vivid color of their flags. Even more breathtaking, a formation of F-16 fighter planes flew over the stadium to participate in the occasion.

Once the game started, there were the usual commercials, but in addition, there were interruptions for news updates on the war in the Gulf.[8]

This example is important for a number of reasons. It demonstrates the power of media to assist in forming a collective consciousness about a world event by using a popular sports event. "It also brought the scholarly commentators on the Gulf War into a new forum—a huge audience of sports fans to bring them 'on board' with the national spirit of support for the war."[9] It used the metaphor of competing teams to subliminally drive home the notion of Americans in a confrontation with Iraqis, cementing the idea of a nonlethal competition. The American government, in a historically successful strategy was assuring its public that it was striking at nonhuman targets with carefully prepared surgical strikes. Americans pride themselves on living in a society where the unquestioned assumption (is) that there is a completely open, free flow of information.

When we add media images to what anthropologists, historians, and geopolitical strategists explain, the information is sometimes skewed to support or affirm a governmental action. While this is not always the case, when it comes to Islam and Muslims, it is usually the case. And from the last example we can see that Muslims are not always innocent in the transaction. Our original question of media was how they determine what we value.

Media specialists say that because Americans believe that media persons, especially documentary and news media persons, tell the truth, portray what is important, and are products of an open information system, we are not likely to question the information that we receive. Thus we value what we are told is important. The power of TV to determine what is important and to literally run the lives of the people who depend on the medium for information is awesome.

Since September 11, 2001, the U.S. government, many Middle East "experts," most television news anchors, and many Christian and Jewish scholars writing on Islam and Muslims have successfully cast Islam as evil and, thus, Muslims as terrorists in the minds of most non-Muslim Americans. One reason for the necessity of threat is given by Samuel Huntington in his most recent text.[10] His thesis is that Americans have lost much of their Anglo-Protestant identity through a series of attempts to engage the multicultural and multireligious society that is America's current state. He then asserts:

> So long as Americans see their nation endangered, they are likely to have a high sense of identity with it. If their perception of threat fades, other identities could again take precedence over national identity.[11]

For professor and government advisor Samuel Huntington, multicultural societies must have an enemy or at least a serious threat amongst them in order to have coherence in the national identity. September 11, 2001, caused such coherence, and its attendant violence. But Professor Huntington laments that the alarm did not last long enough. In this text he targets Latinos. Given enough time, he probably will be able to stir up a frenzy against Latinos but not one as fervent as was achieved with the same history as the war against Islam and Muslims. The threat necessary for sustaining a shared identity asserted by Professor Huntington was present as Anglo-Christian communities came together, overriding their differences to protest the threat.

Who Are Immigrant Arabic-Speaking Muslims?

Arabic speakers hold a unique position among Muslim immigrants in the West and anywhere in the Muslim world. As a transnational community, they are guardians of the language of revelation and primarily responsible for its dissemination. Language retention among religious Arabic-speaking Muslims is unavoidable since prayers and community interaction are daily occurrences. Arabic speakers are also asked to be Arabic teachers, which increases pride in ethnicity and the burden of acquiring special skills. Though Arabic is the language of revelation, the vocabulary of the Qur'an is finite and spoken in an Arabic that the listeners in seventh-century Arabia could understand. Arabic speakers know their particular Arabic dialect and education enables them to pursue knowledge of Arabic literature, philosophy, and law. But authority is derived both from actual knowledge of the Qur'an, *Hadith* literature, and the law, no matter how biased, along with the facility to recite that knowledge on demand. Authority is further cemented as an artifact of lifelong study, making knowledge of Arabic language both a highly sought skill and virtually unattainable.

Consequently, language maintenance is a high priority. Intimacy with the Arabic language has also become a primary consideration for leadership and authority in all the ethnic Muslim communities in the United States. Among Arabic speakers there is a hierarchy of authenticity. Those having first contact with Islam on the Arabian Peninsula are considered the guardians of the

Qur'an and Islamic knowledge. Subsequent converts are ranked by their degree of Arabic language proficiency and attendance in schools in particular places such as Mecca, Medina, and Cairo. For example, Egyptians, Iraqis, and Syrians are converts to Islam and thus once removed from the center of Islam and, therefore, must pass the language test. Tunisians, Algerians, and Moroccans are even further removed from the center as converts and fall lower on the Arabic-speaking proficiency hierarchy. All of this translates into categories of authority and authenticity.

As purveyors of the language of revelation, these Arabic-speaking Muslims had a burden added to the experiences of immigration. Prior colonizations and state formations prevent unity and most times encourage differentiation. The tie that binds, however, is intimacy with the language of revelation that confers authority inside the community and in the religious landscape of America. American media representations of the Muslim world, as mentioned previously, paint a vague picture of the geography of that world.

> Stretching some 5.25 million square miles between the Gulf and the Atlantic, the Arab world is officially composed of twenty-one states and inhabited by a mostly young population expected to number over 200 million before the end of the twentieth century. Besides linking Asia and Africa, it has long served as the gateway to Europe.[12]

Arabic-speaking Muslims in America represent a range of cultures in the Arab world and in the world at large.

7

Arab Muslims in the United States

In 2000, when Muslim residents of the Chicago suburb of Palos Heights attempted to buy a church that had been for sale since March 1998, the community response was fearful.

> Rev. Edward Cronin was in the middle of parish business last February when the pastor of the Reformed Church of Palos Heights (a Chicago suburb) called to tell him that the Reformed congregation finally had a buyer for its building.
>
> A Muslim organization wanted to turn the church into a mosque, the first in the suburb's 41-year history.
>
> "I said, 'O boy. I wonder how our people might react to this,'" recalled Cronin, acknowledging that he, let alone his parishioners at Saint Alexander's Catholic Church, knew very little about the faith.[1]

The encounter in Palos Heights is one in a sequence of interactions in many towns across America that now has a national audience. While the above quotation describes innocent ignorance about a fourteen-centuries-old world religion, ignorance was quickly replaced with hostility toward Islam and Muslims. One alderwoman asked with incredulity: "We all see these movies about the Far East. Do you actually announce [the call to prayer] on a loudspeaker?"[2] Another community leader cast the theologically negative view and called Islam a "heretical" religion.

To prevent this kind of religious presence—having a masjid (mosque) in the area—members of the City Council, along with some residents, hatched a plan to buy out the Muslims. The mayor, however, vetoed this plan, and the battle was begun. As of this writing, the Muslims are suing the township for interfering with the church's sale of its land and then causing a loss of the original offer along with the rescindment of a buyout offer after the controversy began. The church, however, is not countersuing. This event, nevertheless, illustrates the fact that in the year 2000, distrust, dislike, and hostility toward Islam and Muslims is alive and well in the United States. Meanwhile, immigrant American Muslims have remained oblivious to U.S. history.

Many residents of Palos Heights were residents of collar (seamless borders) suburbs of Chicago during the Civil Rights and Black Power movements. Their fears of diversity had forced them out of places like Cicero, Illinois (a collar suburb with a long history of racial intolerance). For many years their lives were relatively racially and religiously homogeneous in the white, Christian enclave of Palos Heights. The immigrant Muslim's pattern of moving into white suburbs in significant numbers was something they had not anticipated. Initially, since the majority of the immigrants were Arab and white in skin color, although they were undesirable, they were few in number without a physical monument to their presence, so they could be tolerated. It was not until these immigrants wanted a place of worship that a fissure appeared in the tolerance, and the stereotypes about Islam and Muslims began to emerge.

Reexamining the quotations from the city's leaders, we can easily see that the city council member relates that her knowledge of Islam and Muslims comes from the movies while another community leader claims that Islam is a heresy. Technically, these two understandings, heresy and movie-based knowledge, are different, but in this case as in other instances, one kind of knowledge affirms another kind. Many Americans understand both kinds of knowledge as legitimate and true representations of Islam and Muslims.

Arabic Speakers in the United States

In the early years of immigration to the United States, most Arab Muslims came from Greater Syria, composed of the contemporary countries of Syria, Jordan, Palestine, and Lebanon.

Though "no religious census has been taken in the United States since 1936, and the figures that year did not include a count of Muslims,"[3] researchers like Adam Lebor assert that

> in fact most of America's Arab population of about 2.5 million are Christians. By far the largest group, over 40 percent of American Muslims, are African American, according to the American Muslim Council. The next largest group, about 25 percent, hails from the Indian sub-continent. Arabs . . . comprise about 12 per cent of America's Muslim population.[4]

The reader should be reminded that these figures have changed with more recent demographic studies but the overall consensus affirms the above quote. Nevertheless, Islam has been understood as Arab. There are twenty-one countries where Arabic is the official language. Immigrant Arab Muslims represent all of them in varying numbers. There are large numbers of Arab Muslims from what was called Greater Syria and Palestine along with significant numbers from Egypt, North Africa, and the Sudan, representing twelve countries.

In the early years of immigration to the United States, many Arabs came as unskilled workers, refugees, or those escaping army conscription to fight with the Turks in various wars or to fight in wars of independence. They primarily settled in the Midwest because of the farmland and manufacturing plants, and also on the East Coast. Each ethnic community, though sharing language, existed in its own subcommunity of shared "home life." There are a few accounts of the lives of these early immigrants.[5] The creation of the state of Israel was the first impetus for the immigration of significant numbers of Arabic speakers from Palestine. The Arab-Israeli War of 1967 led to more immigration as did the *intifada* in the 1980s and the most recent *intifada*. Other Arabic speakers have come with the opening of the door of immigration after 1965.

There are a few studies of Arab Muslims in the United States. One such study, *Islamic Values in the United States* by Yvonne Haddad and Adair Lummis, focuses on the Muslim Arab immigrant community, foregrounding their values.[6] In this study several major themes emerge, such as the intracommunity conflicts, innovations in the role of the imam, and concerns with early assimilation/acculturation and later segregation. Interestingly, these themes remain as priorities. One observation was that the larger the number of immigrants from the same region, the greater the "conscious self-definition along national lines." Arabs, as the earliest of the immigrant Muslim communities until the import of South Asian professionals in the late sixties, have found themselves outnumbered and in competition for leadership and authority among themselves and with South Asians. Their encounters with the general American community as Arabs were once almost nonexistent as they assimilated. Now, recent immigrants have reversed some of that interaction as they desire to maintain their cultural heritage.

American Culture and Arab Culture: Distinctions

Knowledge of the Muslim world, as previously stated, lies in the subconscious of most Americans. Knowledge of America in the Muslim world is filtered through the same kinds of lens—print and broadcast media, experience of the tourist, colonialism, and scholars. Both cultures live at extremes—one at the extreme of "democracy" with its notions of individualism and freedoms and the other in an extreme of chaos and conflict with dreams of a glorious past. Neither culture is critically self-reflective.

> Cultural self-awareness is not always easy since culture is internalized as patterns of thinking and behaving that are believed to be "natural"—simply the way things are.[7]

> The core difficulty in cross-cultural interaction is—simply stated—a failure to recognize relevant cultural differences. Because of superficial stereotyping and the belief that one's own values and behaviors are natural and universal, Americans (and others) at home or abroad often fail to grasp the social dynamic that separates them from their associates.[8]

The notion of individualism is pervasive in American culture and is held to be a virtue, a distinction, and a sign of progressiveness. A market that strives to "satisfy individual desire" drives individualism in American culture. Individual effort is what may have its result in success. It is the individual who needs privacy, and it is the individual whose needs must be respected. Integrity and shame belong to the individual, not to the family. Arabs, on the other hand, have always believed that fate and loyalty to one's family takes precedence over personal needs. The individual has duties and obligations but only after the responsibility to God; all other obligations are to the family. Personal integrity or shame belongs also to the family. Anything an individual does has good or bad consequences for the family. Thus, "a person's dignity, honor and reputation are of paramount importance and no effort should be spared to protect them, especially one's honor."[9] Like South Asian Muslims, Arab Muslims want to convey that sense of dignity and honor, to create a good impression to others. While personal status in the West is understood as what the individual has achieved (either divorced from or married to the family), Arab cultures see individual achievement as family achievement. While this is often seen as rationality versus irrationality, it is in fact about what is valued.

> While cultural assumptions refer to basic beliefs about the nature of reality, cultural values refer to the goodness or desirability of certain actions or attitudes among members of the culture.[10]

Arab culture, not in contradistinction to Western rationality, places a different value on quality and very personalized relationships. It is the relationship that in a real sense drives the quality of work. Because there is the understanding that relationships come with rights and duties, perceptions of situations (attentiveness to the context) override operational procedures and calculability. Arab families could be defined as a web of duties and the basic socioeconomic unit.

Arab children, like other Muslim children, are taught very early to have a profound respect for adults. They are conditioned to greet visitors, shake hands or kiss them on the cheek, and provide a little conversation before disappearing into the house. As in South Asian culture, close family friends are given names of endearment such as aunt or uncle. The behavior of children reflects the family honor and integrity. One major tool of disciplining children is shaming. And while physical punishment is rare, it is used as a last resort. What is right or wrong is neither arbitrary nor fluid. In concurrence with Islamic law, acts are in classes regarding their permissibility—what is known as right behavior by the community over time is acceptable while what is unknown is unacceptable. This applies to acts/behaviors as well as states of being.

Children do not have rights over adults and often express shock at the liberty and understanding of rights asserted by non-Muslim American children regarding tasks as simple as house cleaning or issues such as staying out late at night. One fifteen-year-old first-generation Arab American girl willingly spoke about her confusion.

> I was blown away when I found out girls in my class could say no to their mothers about cleaning or washing dishes, or just not do it. I went to one girlfriend's house after school to work on a report and she actually talked back to her mother. I have never seen this before. Everyone I know expects to help with the cleaning, wash dishes, serve guests, and baby-sit. I once asked my mother why when she asked me to do something and the look on her face was enough to make me feel ashamed. I don't understand how other families let the kids act like adults, although it is interesting.[11]

Unlike South Asian children, Arab children work at early ages in the family-owned business. Though status and wealth are sought, there is an understanding that working builds character and responsibility. Also unlike many South Asian child-rearing practices, in Arab practices there is an absence of a focus on a limited number of professions that entail working for others. Entrepreneurship in the true American fashion is held in high esteem. As children become young adults, however, tradition again is the great influencer as parents begin planning their marriages.

Engagement and Marriage

Like other immigrant Muslims, Arab Muslims prefer arranged marriages inside the same ethnic group but not necessarily within the same family. As with most immigrant Muslim cultures, the romantic notions of the ideal family or love are not priorities—status and security are what counts. Here in the United States, mates often come from different families, usually within the same ethnic group, though there are increasing exceptions to this general state. Since family life is built around the extended family and children are their parents' old-age security, who marries whom is vitally important to the entire family.

Arab Muslims, coming from many countries, are not a monolithic group, even though there are some mores that Arabs have in common that are different from other ethnic groups of Muslims. What can be said definitively is that there is first a concern that children get married and that they preferably marry Arabs from their country, then perhaps Arab Muslims from other countries, European Americans (Muslim or not), and then perhaps other Muslims. No matter who a young adult marries, there is a general understanding that the family needs to approve.

In some families the intended spouses meet and have the opportunity to "size one another up" and say yes or no. In other families parents have the say. In the United States there are a number of variations on the theme. Some women came as new brides of husbands who had been in the United States for some time, earning money and getting settled. Some of these new brides had previously met their husbands and some had not. In other instances, young men raised and educated in the United States have married young women from "back home" and brought them to the United States. Still other couples have met here in the United States or in educational settings in other Western countries. As with all young people, reassurance on issues of well-being comes with knowing about families, status, income, and security.

Since it is understood that men are indeed the heads of families, often with all the decision-making power, it is important that men have good, stable work in a profession or business. Women as the clearly defined head-of-household, and certainly influential in decision making, must be able to manage their homes. They must be able to "keep house" and rear children with Arab values. Children are always desired and the more the better. Again, in contrast to South Asian families, many Arab children grow up, marry, and may move away from parents. Many South Asian couples initially live with one set of parents or very close by in the same neighborhood. Please keep in mind, these characteristics are generalizations, as there are differences in Arab cultures.

The transition to living in America with other Arabs and Muslims of other cultures is both rewarding and taxing. Rearing children and marrying them according to tradition is more difficult in America. Increasingly, keeping marriages together is also a problem. As many parents attempt to encourage traditional values, children are exposed to a worldview that increasingly treats children as if they were adults. In the United States, as children are taught to have an opinion, they also learn that they can make decisions for which only they are responsible, whether that is ultimately true or not. In traditional Arab families, children are taught that they are part of a collective in which the actions of any individual member has good or bad consequences for everyone. While they are individually responsible for their actions, the limitations of their experiences make consultation necessary. The concept of the rugged individual who can hold the opinions of others in disdain is antithetical to Arab (and most third-world) concepts of child-raising. Though these cultural characteristics are typical of Arab families, again, Arabs from different cultures are different in many ways.

Palestinians

Unlike Algerians, who endured the longest (123 years) and certainly one of most brutal colonizations by the French, and also unlike those Arab societies that were occupied by governments who had a resident homeland, the Palestinian experience in the twentieth century is unique. Israelis, fleeing genocide and discrimination in Christian and communist lands, felt the need for a homeland for the safety of their community and decided on Palestine, the home of Arab Christians and Muslims. To insure their safety and with the help of Western powers, Israelis systematically pushed the majority of the Palestinian population out of Jerusalem by either buying or seizing property and building settlements for Jews in all the surrounding areas to ensure space for Jewish immigration. Palestinian outrage at their forced removal from their land and Israel's need for security and space has initiated a cycle of terrorism on both sides that continues unabated.

Though all Arab societies feel aggrieved by the 1948 establishment of the state of Israel, the greatest burden fell on three-quarters of a million Palestinians who were immediately uprooted and dispersed either into refugee camps or into a diaspora. Jordan, Lebanon, Egypt, and Syria have now become home to at least two generations of Palestinians. The enormity of the refugee crisis required the formation of the UNRWA (United Nations Relief and Works Agency) to provide food, clothing, and assist with education. All countries that took in Palestinian refugees, with the exception of Jordan, placed various restrictions on their freedom, causing animosity and the loss of any hope of real settlement. Jordan gave Palestinians citizenship and then found itself at the center of a nascent Palestinian resistance, forcing the Jordanian government to take military action against some of its Palestinian citizens. Palestinians feel that they have been violently ejected from their homes by the Israelis and abandoned by the Arab world in their plight. The establishment of the State of Israel sent steady lines of Palestinian immigrants to America, making this community of Arabic speakers the largest.

Palestinian immigration to the United States has been surrounded with difficulty. In many cases complete families cannot emigrate because of Israeli land-occupation laws. These laws permit the government to confiscate land that is unoccupied for three years. Additionally Palestinians have not given up the fight for the right to live in "Palestine" and to free Palestinians from the camps and diasporas. No matter where Palestinians live outside of Israel and the immediate occupied territories, they are tied to both the idea of Palestine as well as the land itself. As a result, they are unable to separate from "home" though they have relocated. Palestine and the Palestinian cause remain rooted in the heart and mind in a way unknown to other Muslim refugees. A further complicating factor is living in the United States, which supported the establishment of the State of Israel and has continued uncritical support of Israeli violations of international law and UN sanctions.

Stereotyping and the discrimination upon which it is based take a toll on any ethnic community. For Palestinians the additional strain of having been forced out of home is always evident, always present, as they endure the stereotyping and discrimination. This situation keeps alive both support for Palestinian resistance to Israeli occupation and the sense of humiliation and anger.

Early Palestinian transnationals settled in both rural and urban areas of America, especially in the Midwest. Selling goods door-to-door evolved into small family-business ownership and provided a means to assist newer immigrants. Newer immigrants, those who have arrived since 1970, live primarily in major urban areas. Unlike Iranian immigrants, for example, but similar to many early Jewish immigrants, Palestinians opened stores in minority neighborhoods. Many lived for a time in the neighborhoods of their business, moving when either they made enough money to do so or when the community became severely economically depressed. In some large urban areas, families formed enclaves.

Events in Israel, especially since the first *intifada,* have greatly influenced Palestinian political activism in the United States. Recognition of the powerful Israeli lobby in the U.S. government gave rise to Arab-American political groups, some of whose members are both Christian and Muslim. The Arab Anti-Defamation League monitors prejudice and discrimination in media and in public speeches. The Council on American-Islamic Relations emerged to extend the work of the Arab Anti-Defamation League to all Muslims and to assist in the struggle to create a lobby for Palestinian rights overseas. Both of these groups have been active in preparing pamphlets for various aspects of the public sector on Islam and Muslims along with providing legal resolutions to illegal acts against Muslims in the public space.

The special tensions that exist for Palestinian Americans because of their efforts to support families living in refugee camps, small villages in the occupied territories, and organizations that serve them have caused them endless trouble in the United States. Lobbying efforts by Jewish organizations have placed almost all Palestinian groups on the U.S. terrorist list; thus limiting Palestinian American charity and support to families and institutions in Palestine. Because immigrants, regardless of ethnicity, often send or take cash "home," it was relatively easy for the anti-Arab lobbies to argue that all Palestinian monies go to the support of "terrorist" groups and that their charity is criminal. There have been notable consequences; one of which is government surveillance of the Palestinian community. On January 25, 1993, two Arab-American businessmen visiting the Israeli-occupied West Bank were arrested upon arrival for suspicion of supporting militant Islamic groups as they were carrying money to relatives. Instances like this have caused ruptures in the fragile cohesion of the Arabic-speaking community. Some other Arabs have become wary of association with Palestinians because the government will include them in the surveillance. Other American Muslims, perceiving these governmental actions as unconstitutional, have joined protests against such assaults on civil liberties.

Despite these tensions, Palestinians have struggled to take advantage of all the opportunities available in American society. Most children, boys and girls, are encouraged to complete a university education as resources permit. There are high percentages of Palestinians in such professions as medicine, science, law, engineering, and political science. In this way, they have turned adversity into challenge and opportunity. Palestinian women have been at the forefront of most of these efforts just as they were in Palestine.

The contributions of Palestinian women in maintaining family and efforts of resistance to Israeli occupation have been masked by the issues of the Arab-Israeli War itself. Palestinian women have been in the "forefront of institution building, social work, and cultural production."[12] Israeli occupation and confiscation of land forced out those men who were able to find work in other countries, leaving women to head households. Orayb Najjar asserts:

> Israeli occupation has weakened the patriarchal dimension of the family—through land confiscation and forced labor migration; while at the same time reinforcing its necessity as a vehicle of economic and psychological survival, of nationalism and resistance.[13]

Once the family is in the United States, these problems remain as the father must protect the land in Palestine.

Women are also in the forefront of heritage preservation through the conservation of traditional Palestinian crafts, especially embroidery. Palestinian "embroidery is a unique art form with no close parallel in neighboring regions."[14] Memories of villages demolished by Israeli tanks are kindled in the colors, materials, and designs of dresses. The Palestinian Heritage Foundation keeps this art alive in the United States and maintains the collective village memories.

Women have also responded to attempts to decimate the Palestinian population through murders, imprisonment, and deportation by increasing the number of births. Many Palestinian-American Muslims have six to nine children on the average. As Najjar demonstrates, the work of women is complex and vital but it is often omitted in most texts on this crisis although not in the minds of the community.

Palestinian-American children are politicized early. Most of this political education is unavoidable since male family members are constantly forced to return to the land, support family members left behind, and mourn either a new occupation or a death. The effect is best seen in communities where some of the children become disciplinary problems at school. Raising children between two worlds, keeping family together under tremendous stress, and learning about America is an enormous task.

In recalling their first impressions of life in the United States, women had more personal accounts that led to a wide-ranging discussion which included talk of "honor killings." One woman interviewed had been married at fifteen and then moved with her twenty-five-year-old husband to the United States. In recalling her first impressions of the United States, with a broad smile she remembered:

> I got married at fifteen because I wanted to. I was too shy to say no. I lucked out and married a good person. I used to see American girls so free, running around, I liked that. I used to see how free they are, wearing shorts, able to stay out late. I did not know about all the problems they have—going to bed with any man without marriage, drugs, no responsibility. I would never now think what I used to think. I was the first to get married that young in my family. I lived in Ramallah.[15]

Commenting on the issue of "honor killing" which came up as we discussed what happens when girls don't want the mates selected for them, Maryam said,

> I never heard of people who killed their daughters. We hear that it is done, perhaps in remote villages. This is a hidden thing. Why would anyone know that someone killed their daughter when you are trying to keep the honor of the family and leave no stain? If everyone knew, then you would not be able to marry the other daughters off. People don't go around talking about it. I have heard more about it recently here in the United States than I ever did at home.[16]

Though all of the women interviewed denied ever having known a family involved in an honor killing, when asked about an honor killing in St. Louis,

Missouri, everyone remembered. This issue emerged regarding the Palestinian community when on November 6, 1989, Palestina Isa was murdered by her father, Zein Isa, a Palestinian immigrant from the village of Beitin.[17] In St. Louis, the Zein family lived a chaotic life filled with the running of a grocery store, the absence of a father who allegedly belonged to the Abu Nidal Organization, and rigid cultural understandings about women. This story, though very complex, was intertwined with charges and suspicions of espionage, money laundering, travel, and adventure. It also affirmed opinions of the "insanity of Arabs." Maryam said, "this was crazy and all of us were embarrassed." A part of the story that Harris focused on in her book was the father's hatred of African Americans. Palestina Isa's boyfriend was an African-American honors student whom she was with daily. Her seeing him in addition to working outside the family business was more than the father's honor could take, so he and the family conspired to murder her. When asked about "hatred of African Americans" Maryam asserted:

> It is not hate. It's racism just like with white people. If an Egyptian came and asked for my daughter, I would have a problem, or an Indian. You want to fit into society. Now my oldest daughter married a Syrian and I have to explain. There is no reason. Our leaders will say it's fine Islamically, but they don't do it themselves. I am ashamed to say I still feel this way. We (Muslims) are becoming one here but it is still a problem.[18]

On other subjects such as living in the United States, many of the women interviewed agreed that living was difficult because "you never feel you belong here, that people accept you."

> People here in the United States don't know much about people in the world. They are not good at accepting other people for who they are and we don't either. I used to think Americans were just ignorant but I found that we are just as ignorant. We see the papers and a video and think that all Americans are drunks, druggers, and sex crazy. It takes a while to see that most Americans are decent and just don't know others as friends. But we don't make friends either. We live together and don't associate with anybody else unless we work or go to school and then we don't invite people to dinner.[19]

Asking women about how they were raising their children in the United States generated a lot of discussion of terms. Many women said they raised their children "traditionally." *Traditional* meant that girls were "trained to keep immaculate houses, cook, sew, and care for other children in addition to keeping up with schoolwork." One woman explained that in Palestine there was "family all around to help keep children in their place but here you have to try to keep girls traditional." All of the women interviewed complained that their boys did nothing and that this was their fault as mothers. Several women expressed the wish that they had raised their children "Islamically," meaning to see men and women as equal.

Although there is a high level of political activism in the community, it was limited to the Israeli-Arab crises. They did not attend lectures or rallies for other Muslim communities. This partisanship seemed to be the trend for each immigrant community. If an event was held for a crisis in one community, only members of that community were present. Unlike other second- and third-generation young adults, many young adult members of this community are as attached to Palestine as are their parents and grandparents. Many also feel that the inability of the community to lobby the U.S. government to be fair to Palestinians makes their U.S. home an insecure place.

Egyptians

While Arabs in general understand themselves to be at the center of Islam, Egyptians see themselves additionally as part of the beginning of world civilization. This self-perception has several thousand years of history as evidence. Pyramids, the Sphinx, thousand-year-old mummies, intrigue and mystery are all a vital part of Egypt's past and present. Egypt houses the oldest university in civilization, al-Azhar—the most prestigious university in the Muslim world. For 2,284 years, foreigners ruled Egypt without interruption, with Egyptian governance emerging only with the "abdication" of King Farouk in 1952.

Today Egypt is a country where a four-thousand-year-old past mingles intimately with the new. Though Egypt is large, most of it is desert. Out of approximately 386,900 square miles, only a tiny portion, less than one-third, is arable land. The Nile Valley supports the population, over seventy million and quickly growing, on about 5 percent of the land. Egyptians made particularly good use of their desert. The tombs of Pharaohs, ancient buildings, and other monuments survived thousands of years here because of climatic conditions. Crowded, noisy, grand, and alluring is Egypt's most famous city, Cairo. The population in greater Cairo in the 1991 census was 14 million, with an annual growth rate of one million, all living on the same percentage of the land. Egypt produces more than a hundred thousand university graduates every year, though there are few jobs and a crippling literacy rate of 48–50 percent.

Islam transformed Egypt in 642 C.E. supplanting Christianity. By 706 C.E. Arabic was the official language. In almost fifty years, contemporary Egypt has had only three leaders—Gamal Abd al-Nasser, Anwar Sadat, and the current president, Husni Mubarak. Citizens have embraced, or at least lived under, socialism, unregulated capitalism, and military repression. Egyptians have experienced radical change from Nasser's Russian-backed socialism that nationalized institutions and industries; through Sadat's Western unregulated capitalism, which caused deindustrialization, falling incomes, and increased bureaucracy; and Mubarak's military rule of twenty years in a state of emergency.

Currently, the government owns almost all large industry and controls much of the activity in the private sector. Precisely because the government either owns or controls every entity including industry, rents, and agricultural produce, and a bureaucracy that is burdened beyond repair, Egypt is a country of constant dis-ease. A recent study stated that the average Egyptian bureaucrat works a total of twenty-seven minutes per day, making the average transaction a nightmare. The government is the largest employer, with so many employees overseeing each aspect of every encounter that redundancy threatens to wipe out the institutions. Many of these employees just have a job. They earn very little in wages but have prestige because they are a part of the government and can assist or stall any endeavor. Efforts by foreign investors and the World Bank to reverse this economic quagmire have only succeeded in filling the bank accounts of a privileged few and further increased the disparity in earnings between the wealthy and the poor.

Egypt, despite continual internal political and economic chaos, played a pivotal role in the Arab-Israeli War of 1967. Israel attacked Egypt in 1967 and decisively gained control of critical territory, turning a smoldering Arab bitterness into hostility. Though the West, particularly the United States, supports Egypt's current government, the continuing Israeli occupation of its neighbor, Palestine, makes Egypt a volatile place under its own brutal state of emergency, spurring emigration.

Arab Americans of Egyptian ancestry who are Muslim, sometimes classified in old immigration records as Syrian along with Palestinians, came in large numbers to the United States in the 1960s.[20] The high and low tides of American-Egyptian relations, largely based on Egypt's attitude toward Israel, have the largest influence on Egyptian immigration quotas. These Arabic speakers' American experience has largely been that of other Arabic speakers, filled with stereotypes and discrimination, yet they have actively integrated themselves into this society.

The voices of Arab Americans who are Christian have been the loudest regarding issues of discrimination, and they have been heard in fields of science, research, and literature. Fortunately or unfortunately, their voices as Christians have been overshadowed by the prevailing stereotype that all Arabs are Muslims.

The Sudanese

The Sudan is Africa's largest country with the continent's longest running civil war. In 2000 its population was estimated at thirty-five million. Sunni Islam is the dominant religion, though Muslims are generally located in the north of the country. Sudan won its independence from both Egypt and the United Kingdom in 1956. Culturally it is a loose confederation of almost six hundred tribes who have Arabic as their common language. Many Sudanese have emigrated to America seeking better education and more opportunities for careers. As members of two Muslim communities—African and Arabic speaking, these Muslims have some unique difficulties regarding race and language.

Sudanese-descended Arab Americans are generally exempt from the stereotypes and discriminations directly aimed at other Arab Americans because of their color. They are, however, exposed to American racism that is principally focused on blacks. Their presence in Arab circles is tenuous as they are truly Arabic speakers but also black. Most Sudanese, despite the racial problems, settle in predominantly Arab communities, though their interactions with African Americans are extensive. As the Sudanese-American community is small, their potential leadership and authority is often masked by other larger Arab communities. Children in these communities often have ambiguous identities living in the United States. They are seen as African Americans who speak Arabic.

> I remember when I was in elementary school, on the first day of school when I was in the sixth grade. The teacher was a very pretty white woman who had a wonderful voice. She called the roll and fumbled my name then looked at me and said, "What are you?" I said, "A girl?" She decided I was giving a smart answer and said, "Don't try to be funny." In my class were white, black, and Latino kids. She put me with another Sudani girl in the black group. We started talking (in Arabic) and then she was angry. I did not understand. She said we were pretending to be black and she was not going to have us talking so she couldn't understand. She separated us and left me in the black group and put the other girl in the Latino group. When she finally asked where we were from and we said America, that did it. She was hostile for the rest of the school term. She did find out that our parents were from the Sudan and then we were just Africans even though different than her picture of Africa.[21]

> My parents put us in the Islamic school in our community. All the kids except for about seven were Arab. They just called us "niggers" all the time. The teachers did nothing to stop them and I just got tired and begged to be put into a public school. Finally, my parents said okay. Now I just hang

> out with the black kids and everything is fine. I speak Arabic at home and in the mosque.[22]

Sudanese Muslims have not been either politically or socially active in the public space of America. Rarely do they participate in interreligious dialogues or interfaith meetings. Most in the community came to the United States as students in various fields such as medicine, finance, computer science, management, and engineering. Many were male and returned home to marry women who were uneducated and from rural areas. Unable to speak English and with little if any formal education, most of those women congregate among themselves, but not even with other Arabic speakers, as they have little in common. The American existence for many of these families is marginal, though they are continuously making valuable contributions to society.

Because of the racial categories in the United States, Sudanese-American Muslims who dress like many in America are considered black in the public space and are treated as such. Within the Muslim community their position is also ambiguous. Sudanese Muslims are renowned in the Arabic-speaking world for their command of Arabic, but here in the United States, the guardians and teachers of the language are "white" Arabs. Sudanese Muslims are also distinguished for their piety and hospitality, but here in the United States they are rarely religious instructors or leaders of the mosque. In effect many of their talents are not used by the Muslim community itself. As just another group of African descended Americans, many have had difficulty distinguishing themselves as Arabic speakers.

8

Iranian Muslim Immigrants

The Philosopher Poets

When anyone in America thinks of Islam or immigrant Muslims, they usually think of Arabs and the Middle East. When there is mention of Shi'ite Islam, few Americans know anything unless reminded of Iran and none as we have seen, think of South Asian Shi'ite Muslims. Iran is not the only nation with a Shi'ite majority, there are also Shi'ite majorities in Iraq (55 percent) and Bahrain (70 percent), though United States media portrays a homogenous and majority Sunni community in all these countries.[1] There are however, significant numbers of Iranian Muslims in America who are Shi'ite. The United States lists Iran as one of the "terrorist Muslim states" where people are "fanatically" religious and therefore violent causing American Shi'ite Muslims to remain largely quietist. Many Sunni Muslims refuse to acknowledge them as Muslims at all, sustaining centuries' old arguments. To Shi'ite Muslims however, though a minority in Islam, they are the "real" Muslims.

Islam became the official religion in Persia in 1501 C.E. Iran became a modern state, officially inaugurated in 1935, and the Islamic Republic of Iran in 1979. It is the only Shi'ite Islamic state in the world.

> It is necessary to present the integral Shi'ite tradition as a major branch of Islam: its doctrines, intellectual life, religious practices, and spirituality. Shi'ism has been concerned with the oppressed and the downtrodden, but for many centuries it also has been the religion of the majority and the ruling powers in several parts of the Islamic world.[2]

Iran became the Islamic Republic of Iran in 1979, with almost seventy million people who have a life expectancy of about seventy years. The country is 89 percent Shi'ite, 10 percent Sunni, with an overall literacy rate of 72 percent. Every four years a new president is elected, and the voting ratio is considerably higher than that of the United States from a truly multiparty system.

A Brief Historical Overview of Religion in Persia

In the sixth century B.C.E. Zarathustra (Zoroaster in Greek), a great prophet of Persia brought the message of a supreme God, Ahura Mazda, who commanded all humans to join the forces of good in the struggle against the forces of evil. This message became the religion of the empire for twelve centuries. Muslims conquered Persia in the seventh century C.E. and the Zoroastrian tradition survived for eight centuries longer, then all but disappeared as many gradually accepted Islam. Today there are less than twenty thousand Zoroastrians living in Iran. Some migrated to India and recently some one thousand are immigrants to the United States. In India and Pakistan, Zoroastrians are also called Parses. Along with Zoroastrians, Jews have lived in Persia for at least thirteen centuries.

Iranian Jews are said to be one of the "Ten Lost Tribes of Israel" mentioned in biblical records, and Jewish chronicles are full of accounts of massacres, forced conversions, and mistreatment.[3] Reza Shah was the first Iranian monarch that paid tribute to the Jewish community and thus is regarded by them with some respect. When Israel became a state in 1948, thousands (estimated at about forty thousands) of Iranian Jews emigrated but some remained. One of those Jews who emigrated was Ehud Barak who became a prime minister of Israel. When all the other Muslim countries in the region expelled their Jewish citizens in protest of the formation of the State of Israel, Iran did not. Almost half of those remaining Iranian Jews (about forty thousand) emigrated to the United States and today form part of the diverse American Iranian community along with part of the American Jewish community. In the United States they have set up organizations such as The Council of Iranian American Jewish Organizations and the Iranian American Jewish Federation.

Most of Iran's Christians are either Orthodox Christians (Assyrians) or Protestant Evangelicals. The history of Christianity in Iran during modern times is much like that of the Iranian Jewish community. Many in this community also emigrated to the United States and form part of the American Iranian community. Like the South Asian challenge of the Ahmadiyyah community, Iranian Islam also experienced internal resistance to orthodoxy. This resistance came in the form of the Bahá'i community.

On May 23, 1844, in Shiraz, Persia, it was announced that there would be the imminent appearance of another Messenger of God. Bahá'u'lláh understood himself as the prophet of civilization. At the core of Bahá'i understanding is the notion that "humanity is one single race and the day has come for its unification in one global society."[4] Considered a heresy to Islam, believers in this community were severely persecuted and most live outside of Iran today though some remain. It is important to note that the burial place of Bahá'u'lláh is in Haifa, Israel and the Israeli government permits pilgrimage there no more than once every ten years. This is considered a true restraint on religious practice. Many

Bahá'i add to the United States' Iranian community. The dominant religious tradition in Iran however, is Shi'ite Islam.

Shi'ism begins with the family of the prophet Muhammad (pbuh); his cousin ʿAli in particular. It is widely understood that ʿAli, the first male convert to Islam, as the cousin and son-in-law of the Prophet (pbuh) spent all of his time under his tutelage. Living in the household of the Prophet (pbuh) gave ʿAli unprecedented access to knowledge of the revelation and the private behavior of the Prophet (pbuh). Given ʿAli's closeness to the prophet of Islam and an assertion by the Prophet (pbuh) in a lecture given at Ghadir al-Khumm (a place between Mecca and Medina) that states:

> I shall soon depart to Allah, to be concealed from you, and bidding farewell to this world. I am leaving amongst you the Book of Allah and my Itrat. And if you follow this you will never go astray. These both would never be separated until they meet me at the fountain of Kawthar [that is, in paradise].[5]

It is reported that the Prophet (pbuh) took ʿAli's hand, raised it and said,

> Whoever has me as his Maula has ʿAli as his Maula. O' Allah love those who love ʿAli and be an enemy to his enemies. Help those who assist him and frustrate those who oppose him.[6]

For Shi'ite Muslims, this is a clear and indisputable appointment of ʿAli as the successor not to prophethood but to leadership of the community of believers after the death of the Prophet (pbuh). For Sunni Muslims, this is a celebration of the relationship between the Prophet (pbuh) and his cousin/son-in-law. And this is where the difference between Sunni and Shi'ite Islam begins.

At the death of the prophet Muhammad (pbuh), while ʿAli was preparing the Prophet's (pbuh) body for the funeral prayer and burial, companions of the Prophet (pbuh) elected a leader from among them to lead the community. Although this choice was contested, it was thought that it was better to let the choice stand rather than cause chaos in the community. ʿAli did not become leader of the community until twenty-four or twenty-five years later and met with stiff opposition, not to his character but to his leadership. By the time ʿAli took the position, corruption and mistrust were part of the leadership. ʿAli found himself besieged by several local contenders for leadership and a community of relatives of the last Khalifa, located in Damascus. On the nineteenth of Ramadan in the year 40 A.H.(673 C.E.), five years after he assumed leadership, while he was praying in the mosque at Kufa, ʿAli was murdered with a poisoned sword. His two sons, Hasan and Hossein, survived him.

The elder son, Hasan, made concessions to the opposing party and withdrew to live and die in Medina, while the younger son, Hossein, rose to become a resistance leader. On the tenth of Muharram, after days of siege and demands to submit, Hossein fought to a horrible death by decapitation. His head was taken on a platter to Damascus while his body was trampled. This massacre and Hossein's subsequent martyrdom became "the prototype of every struggle for justice, every suffering." The rejection of the Prophet's (pbuh) wishes for leadership, along with the murder of ʿAli and his son—the grandson of the Prophet (pbuh), are events that occupy a central place in the Shiʾite identity. These crimes against the family of the prophet of Islam are commemorated on several of the special holidays among Shiʾite Muslims.

Shiʾism, over the last fourteen centuries, developed its own sciences of Qurʾanic interpretation and *Hadith* literature along with metaphysics, theology, and law. In this branch of Islam, *Hadith* includes the sayings and actions of the prophet Muhammad (pbuh) and ʿAli and also those of the imams (divinely guided leaders). The subject of inquiry in this chapter is Iranian Muslim immigrants. Thus, we will explore Twelve-Imam Shiʾism, the largest community of Shiʾites and the faith of most Iranian Muslims. There are two other groups here in America—one, the Ismaʿili, which we examined in the chapter on South Asian Muslims, and a much smaller group, the Zaydi, who we will not explore because of their minuscule numbers in the United States. A brief look at some of the thought and institutions in Shiʾite Islam will give us background for exploring the foundations of the Iranian Muslim community.

Beliefs and Practices

The word *Shiʾi*, "has come to be accepted as the designation of those Muslims who are followers of ʿAli (nephew and son-in-law of the prophet Muhammad [pbuh]) who was the Prophet's choice for his successor and who is second in allegiance only to Muhammad." Shiʾite Muslims believe the Qurʾan to be the last revelation to humanity and that Muhammad was the last prophet sent to humankind. The Shiʾite interpretation of the leadership centers on the belief that the Imams possess the hidden, esoteric knowledge of the Qurʾanic verses[7] given to them through divine inspiration. According to Moojan Momen:

> Much confusion has arisen due to the use of the word *Shiʾi* to describe persons of very widely differing opinions. To demonstrate this more clearly, two terms should be defined. Firstly, political Shiʾism: this indicates a belief that the members of the house of Hashim (House of the Prophet) are the people most worthy of holding political authority in the Islamic community, but no belief in any particular religious station for

> this family. Secondly, religious Shi'ism: this indicates a belief that particular members of the house of Hashim are in receipt of divine inspiration and are thus the channel of God's guidance to men whether or not they hold de facto political authority.[8]

Shi'ite Muslims believe that human fallibility is such that an ordinary man as leader would mix his own familiar or cultural views with the real meaning of the Qur'an. Thus only the divinely inspired have the ability to glean the full meaning as they master the method of the household of the Prophet (pbuh). The ordinary person can understand the outward meanings (the obvious) and should leave the inward aspects to the imams. While Shi'ite Muslims believe that *Hadith* literature is valid, they question the corruption and lack of vigilance in guarding them throughout history. They insist that Muslims must not slip into a higher regard for *Hadith* literature than for the Qur'an itself. Therefore, in addition to checking the chain of transmission of a *Hadith* (saying of the prophet Muhammad [pbuh] or a witnessed action of his) there must be a correlation between the texts of the *Hadith* with the Qur'an as a necessary condition for its validity.

The imams, for their exemplary sayings and conduct, are the third source of authority in Shi'ism, after the Qur'an and the *Hadith*. For twelve-imam Shi'ites, the twelfth imam, Imam Mohammad al-Mahdi, went into occultation in 874 C.E. Since this date, the period of the Great Occultation is in place, an era that will last until the end of time. During this period, the

> mullahs meet the theological needs without aspiring to take the Imam's place. Moreover, as the Imam is supposedly alive, legal doctrines are not frozen in immutable positions, but can produce new answers in response to new situations: the "gate of interpretation" [*bab al-ejtehad*] is open.[9]

Scholars agree that one outstanding feature of Shi'ism is an attitude of mind that refuses to admit that majority opinion is necessarily true or right. In this frame of mind, they believe that consensus of the people, long extolled though rarely activated by Sunni Muslims, is only valid when it includes the rightly guided opinion of the imam. Since the imam went into occultation in the ninth century, the *ulema* (learned class) have given religious guidance.

Given the fact that on the fundamental practices of faith, Shi'ite Islam has little difference with Sunni Islam, this text treats Shi'ite Islam as a branch of Islam rather than a sect.[10] All religious Shi'ite observe the basic practices of prayer, fasting, charity, and pilgrimage. Holidays revolve around unique Shi'ite history in addition to the three holidays—Feast at end of Ramadan, Feast at end of Hajj, and the Prophet's (pbuh) birthday—which they share with Sunni Muslims.

The Iranian Revolution and the Emergence of the Islamic Republic of Iran

Colonel Reza Khan founded the Pahlavi dynasty in 1921 after a coup d'etat against the Qajar king. During the reign of the Qajar, Iran was colonized by both Britain and Russia. Citizens rose up and supported the military rule of the first of the khans as an alternative to the perceived backwardness of the king. Twenty years later, the Allied forces invaded Iran and made Pahlavi rule unstable. After five years of protracted struggle and challenge, the Pahlavis were back in control until the shah decided to make Iran a virtual colony of the United States. Most of the West was caught totally by surprise at the overthrow of the shah having been unaware of the seriousness of the Iranians' discontent even though U.S. and British intelligence claimed to be the best in the world. This was not a revolution only of the masses. Iranians of all classes participated as the shah was stripped of his throne and the United States lost power in Iran. Though many Iranians did not want an Islamic state, most did not want the shah to remain in power. Iranians had experienced America's interference with their government when the shah had the legislative assembly pass a law that gave American military personnel serving in Iran diplomatic immunity, thus freeing them to commit crimes with impunity. In addition the CIA actively supported the shah against a challenge from Mohamed Mossadegh, a ranking member of the government. This outrageous act, of a foreign power moving to assassinate a leader of another country, offended every Iranian. Such acts fomented a rebellion that would eventually bring about the revolution.

By 1962 such acts as banning the veiling of women, ignoring the strife of the masses, and increasingly giving the West more control over the country, helped lead to a mass uprising, while the year 1979 witnessed a full revolution. Under the leadership of the Ayatollah Khomeini, from exile in France, the shah was overthrown and the Islamic Republic of Iran was born. This birth was precipitated by the students' seizure of the American embassy in Tehran when the United States gave the shah sanctuary against the demands of the majority of the Iranian people. The Ayatollah Khomeini returned triumphantly to Iran as soon as the shah was deposed. The Ayatollah Khomeini was named "man of the year" by *Time* magazine in 1980 as *Time* editors asserted, "The Iranian revolution threatened to upset the world balance of power more than any political event since Hitler's conquest of Europe."

On Valentine's Day, 1979, after repeated demands that the United States force the shah to return to Iran to stand trial and return to the people the millions of dollars he stole, students overran the U.S. embassy, seizing seventy employees and holding them for two days. Without positive response from the United States, on November 4, 1979, students again stormed the embassy and took sixty-six hostages. Immediately TV newscasts began twenty-four-hour a day, seven days a week on-the-scene coverage with pictures of the crisis. Most scholars agree that the nightly TV "specials" on the crisis added to the emotional response of the American masses. As Iranians were seen shouting "death to America and death to the shah," Americans were buying and burning Iranian flags.

While Iranian Americans watched in horror, Americans, confused by the threatening images of Iranians constantly on the television, reacted. Some Iranians lost their jobs; many had their property vandalized and children of Iranian descent were harassed at school. The crisis lasted 444 days, and as one editor asserted, "images from Tehran are forever burned into the American psyche," even nineteen years later.[11] The United States, after having imposed full economic sanctions on Iran for a few years, lifted some of them in order to buy oil only to impose them again after 1996. The sanctions continue up to the present. No matter what the government does, those old enough to remember will not forget women in the streets of Tehran with black cloaks shouting, "death to the United States." Iranian Americans in some ways continue to be associated with the hostage crisis into the twenty-first century. Nevertheless, Iranian Americans are prospering and giving America some of the best of Persian culture though they remain alienated in many ways.

The Persian concept of *ghorbat* describes the strangeness of being physically removed from home and the accompanying intense intellectual and emotional alienation. After the hostage crisis and Iranian Revolution, many Iranian immigrants found themselves worried about their home country and its turmoil and, simultaneously, their safety in the United States. For those old enough to have experienced both the regime of the shah and some of the Islamic Republic, their identity problems were already in crisis. The Pahlavi regime had Persianized Iran, meaning that they celebrated pre-Islamic Persian culture and secularism in every aspect of life. The language of choice was Persian rather than Arabic. The culture was Persian and secular. The Revolution moved swiftly to reclaim Islam in all aspects by cleansing the culture of secularism and restoring Arabic as the language of choice. For those Iranian immigrants, made schizophrenic by these cultural changes, American life became even more difficult as they fought off the backlash of the hostage crisis, leading to a kind of stupor. Large numbers of Iranian Muslims began calling themselves Persians, knowing that many Americans do not really know that Iran and Persia are the same place. Still other Iranians made even greater attempts at either assimilation with abandon, or segregation in small Iranian communities. They limited their interactions with other Americans to the necessity of conversation at work or school. Iranian immigrants who had lived under the shah or the Islamic Republic in a culture of fear are now citizens careful in their conversations and actions as immigrants in the United States.

> Just watching the news made me terrified. They showed the same footage of Muslim women in the streets shouting death to America thousands of times. The news commentators made Iranians seem like animals that moved around in herds. At my job people were asking each other what an Iranian name looked like so that they could find them. Most of my co-workers were hostile to any of us who were not blond and blue-eyed or known to be "pure" Americans. My son's teacher pointed out to the class that he was Iranian and should explain to the class why his people were so vicious and blood-thirsty. Can you imagine![12]

Iranians did not know that Americans did not know of the rage Iranians felt at a quarter of a century of American support for the totalitarian regime of the Shah. American government foreign policy is not common knowledge to many Americans. For many watching their televisions, the hostage crisis was just an act of terrorism led by irrational people whose religion was violent.

Iranian Muslims in America: A Community of Exiles

Many Iranian Muslims are still in the process of settling in, even though they are not new to the United States. Ali Modarresi asserts that, "between 1891 and 1960, some 5,204 Iranians (religion unknown) immigrated to the United States." Here the category of exile is determining because even though they are involved in transnational networks, the families can not go to the root culture at will. Of course this number increased exponentially until the revolution in 1979. But the fact of the revolution did increase their immigration to and exile in America. Many Iranian immigrants are highly skilled and "according to the 1990 census the average income of Iranians was $36,800/year."[13]

There are no reliable statistics on how many Iranians live in the United States because records kept on country of origin leave out the offspring of those immigrants and no records are kept on religion. Additionally, Armenians and Assyrians are not counted as Iranian even when that is their country of origin. The census shows that the largest numbers of Iranians came to the United States during the years 1950–1977 and 1979–1986. Muslims form the largest single religious group, but this is a group with a high level of secularism. A 1991 study revealed that only 2 percent admitted that they observed all religious practices. The mother tongue is Persian for all ethnic Persians with the exception of Armenians. And in the United States, Persians of all faiths talk to one another, unlike keeping the boundaries in Iran. Royalists, who desire restoration of some form of constitutional monarchy in Iran, are the largest political group although many say that some form of democracy is really the goal. But until Iranian society's climate changes toward tolerance of its religious and intellectual diversity, the state of exile remains for many Iranian Americans.

The Story of Exile

Mahnaz Afkhami begins her personal narrative:

> I am an exile. I have been in exile for fifteen years. I have been forced to stay out of my own country, Iran, because of my work for women's rights. The charges against me are "corruption on earth" and "warring with God." Being charged in the Islamic Republic of Iran is being convicted.[14]

In the introduction to his text, Hamid Naficy laments:

> What is reality? What do we know? How do we know the things we think we know? Separation from you is in fact a series of separations. Like links in a chain: separation from the earth—that dry, cruel, and yet nurturing earth of the homeland; separation from the fragrance of spices in the bazaars and from the smell of urine on the mud walls outside the mosques; separation from the native language and the control that is gradually diminishing. Separation from childhood and from the places of childhood; separation from mother . . .[15]

Both Afkhami and Naficy introduce us to some of the most profound experiences of a special kind of immigrant—the exiled. Naficy asserts that "exile is a special case of transnational and postcolonial discourse."

Exiles, as we know, can be voluntary or involuntary. Exiles may also be temporary immigrants—initially coming to the West to take advantage of opportunity. But unlike other immigrants, they cannot voluntarily go home or they fear for their lives if they do go home. Exiles generally are those whom the motherland deemed unfit citizens or criminals, or those whose protests and resistance to the social order drove them to seek a space outside of the motherland. Regardless of the path, many Iranians consider themselves exiled and victimized. Whether the sense of victimization comes from protests over the shah's regime or the birth of the Islamic Republic, there is a profound sense of separation and loss, and denial of both.

> You shun contact with all those healthy, normal natives who are going about their business as if the world is a safe, secure, and permanent place, a piece of which belongs to them by birthright. You work frantically to retain the memory and to reconstruct the past.[16]

> If there is a dinner party at an Iranian home, the only persons present will be Iranians. Sometimes there are two white people present. The only conversation is about Iran.[17]

Expressions of confusion, loneliness, and mourning filter into conversations regardless of the original context, where the longing only ends with death. However, this mournful state has not limited Iranian contributions to American life, though largely invisible. The reason for this lies again in the general perception that all Muslims are Arab. Those people shouting "death to America" are perceived as Arabs not Iranians even though, if asked, some Americans know that Iranians are not Arabs. Ironically, those Muslims attacked in response to the hostage situation in Iran in 1979 were mostly Arab Muslims not Iranians. Many Iranians, however, exist in a chaotic psychological stupor. Some Iranians were in the United States on various kinds of business when the hostage crisis occurred. They found themselves unable to return home. Others out in the world who had been active in various reform movements or who had been owners of large amounts of property or businesses found themselves stripped of their citizenship and passports.[18] They found that they had a new home and an old self.

As with most immigrants, the preservation of culture is a priority, and Iranians are known for their love of poetry and prose. Persian is a class-conscious language where "the vocabulary chosen is based on the station"[19] of the conversants. Probably because of the nature of their language and its most evident product, poetry, Iranians tend to be very introspective and sedate. As with most cultures outside the West, life in Iran revolves around family, which is patriarchal with many cultural constructs around class. The pace of life reflects the attention given to family, crafts, and poetry. Food preparation and consumption reflects this also. Iranian food and the mealtimes themselves are special.

> Breakfast is Persian tea sweetened with sugar. Fresh-baked bread, usually flat bread, with Feta cheese and there are many kinds. Butter and a whole variety of jams and jellies. That would be breakfast. And you can also have a hot-meal breakfast, it could be lamb or other meat that had been stewing all night. It depends.
>
> But the main meal in Iran remains lunch. A typical lunch, a preferred lunch, definitely has rice in it. Persians eat more rice than Chinese people. There is a whole variety of different kinds of rice. But essentially rice is of two kinds, plain rice that is mixed with some kind of meat or vegetables, similar to Chinese food. Then there is a rice that is made with meat and vegetables baked together. The first kind is *chello* and the second is *pullo.* Rice is definitely a mainstay. It's like the potato of Western meals.

> Supper is usually eaten real late. It could be even eleven or twelve [p.m.]. If it's a big gathering then you have variety and heavy meals. But usually dinner is a lighter meal, you have cheese, cut-up fresh vegetables, cucumbers, tomatoes, a lot of yogurt dishes with walnuts, raisins, mint, etcetera.[20]

Mealtime is a time of family gathering and exchange of news, and lunches are at least one and one-half hours. This is one part of "being home" that is sorely missed and every effort is made to keep some mealtimes the same.

There is little literature on Iranians in the United States but that situation is changing as Iranian Americans are now writing autobiographies and short stories of exile.[21] After prolonged discrimination in the United States and failure to repair U.S. relations with Iran, Iranians began in the late 1990s to assert themselves politically. They moved from "legal" citizenship to the ground level of "real" citizenship without investing in "effective" citizenship. The absence of the full process may not be beneficial to the success of the community in the future. One clear political assertion was a letter written to then President Clinton written as a full-page notice in the *New York Times*.

> Dear Mr. President,
>
> There are more than one million first and second generation Iranians and Iranian-Americans residing in this country. They are law-abiding and hardworking citizens and permanent residents of the United States, independent of and unaffiliated with any governmental policies or actions. They come from various religious and socioeconomic backgrounds, they are productive and successful men and women in business, respected teachers and university professors, and highly qualified professionals such as doctors, lawyers, and engineers; they are students attending some of the most prestigious colleges and universities across this country.
>
> Mr. President, Iranians are proud people; they are proud of their heritage of a rich civilization that for thousands of years has contributed to the progress of the family of man and love for humanity. Yet, in the current political landscape, we are being touted as a nation with a "behavior" problem, which does not hesitate to commit acts of violence. This is an offensive, false, and misleading generalization.[22]

Though Iranians lobbied to end sanctions on trade with Iran, how much political participation Iranian Muslims will have in the future is a question. It probably will not be a function of the Iranian community settling in, rather more a question of whether they choose to join other Muslims on a consensus of issues;

or tackle only those issues that affect them based on their "homeland"; or enable them to become "effective" citizens. Regardless of the level of political participation they choose, it is probable that their fate will always be associated with the Iranian Revolution and the Hostage Crisis.

Interviews reveal that there are several philosophical positions among this group on a range of issues, especially regarding the Islamic Revolution. Those Iranians who came to the United States prior to the revolution came mostly to further their education or to share their skills in professions such as engineering and medicine on an everyday basis with other Americans. Most of these Muslim Iranians consider themselves invested in America with a longing for the smells and sights of home. These professionals may be very religious or completely secular. Most, if not all of them, were not in support of the revolution as it compromised their wealth and land holdings and conversely, they were definitely not in favor of theocracy.

Among those who support the revolution are student groups who are themselves supported in some way by the Islamic Republic of Iran, and a few who believe that Islam must be preserved in the face of a western takeover. There are many more Americans of Iranian descent who loathe the American takeover of their country and its resources. Simultaneously, there are those who loathe the idea of a theocracy. They are ambivalent about its success since the development of the Islamic Republic of Iran is still very much in process and now has some moderate leadership. Then there are those such as the National Council of Resistance, who see no good in the present or past government in Iran.

The National Council of Resistance and the National Liberation Army of the People's Mujahideen (Mujahideen e-Khalq) of Iran have offices in Washington D.C. Massoud Rajavi leads the NLA while his wife, Maryam, has been elected (in 1993) the future president of Iran. Their actual army camp is located on the Iran-Iraq border some sixty miles north of Baghdad. One unique, overwhelming presence in this community is that of women in prominent positions, especially those who lead the armed forces. They report that women "comprise greater than 70 percent of the officer corps and one-third of the rank and file"[23] in an army that claims thirty thousand soldiers. The representatives of this resistance in Washington are veiled, personable women who are committed to the overthrow of the current Iranian government. They have organized a number of conferences here in the United States and supported a number of American Muslim women to attend conferences at their Paris headquarters. This group, however, is not without its skeptics and detractors. When asked, one Iranian American asserted that this group had a different purpose.

> I've heard about them and I am aware that they belong to a terrorist organization. Unfortunately, the United States government and the Israeli

> government from behind the scenes support them and now even the U.S. government has come to realize that they should not support them. Incidentally, it should be pointed out that before the Islamic Revolution in Iran, the only terrorist organization in Iran that actively killed American officials in Iran is the same group and when the revolution happened and the people of Iran overthrew the dictatorial, secular dictatorship in Iran, this group after about one or two years fell in foul with the developing government. Western powers felt that helping the enemy of my enemy will help me. There are many other groups as well. I find them totally insignificant. They have played no role except every once in awhile to go and throw a hand grenade or burn some government building. But other than that they are irrelevant.[24]

Though considered a personality cult by some, a terrorist organization by others, this group has attracted audiences to listen to their side of the story, thus furthering inquiry on the current state of affairs in Iran. These gatherings have led some non-Muslim Americans to ask about Persian/Iranian culture. What they find is a culture that is alive and vibrant though almost underground in the West.

Like other Muslims, Iranians see U.S. power over the Muslim world in their control over the United Nations and the World Bank. Many Iranians are in awe of the United States's uncritical support of Israel and the amount of American taxpayer dollars that are sent to "support the elimination of Palestinians."[25] Also, as with other Muslims, the prevailing attitude of Iranian Muslims toward American culture, whether immigrant or indigenous, is one of ambivalence.

> A conversation with virtually any Muslim will show that the omnipresence of alcohol, drug addiction, nudity on television and in movies, homosexuality, sexual intercourse outside marriage, and the constant drive for wealth in the United States are all viewed as signs of an immoral society and a decaying nation. On the other hand, immigrant Muslims have benefited from the opportunities found in the United States.[26]

Nevertheless, even in exile, Iranians have created an Iranian-American culture that preserves what is culturally important—poetry, music, theater, and family continuity. With large numbers of Iranians living on the West Coast, many Iranian-owned businesses serve their cultural needs. Kereshmeh Records, based in Los Angeles, provides all kinds of Persian music from classical to regional—*Bakhshi, Korasan, Kurdistan* and *Radef.* There is an online Persian and Iranian all-music radio station, www.parsradio.com along with a source for Iranian videos—www.iranianmovies.com, which provides videos on classical and contemporary poets, comedy, soccer, dance, and even recent videos shown in Iran. Iranian Muslims (and certainly all Iranian immigrants) indeed have a unique experience with the United States because of the Iranian Revolution. Nevertheless, the living goes on and it is a struggle to maintain culture, especially in institutions like marriage. Although some marriages have incorporated an American "part," there is still the Iranian flavor.

As with most immigrants, Iranian Muslims prefer to marry within their community but are not as adamant as other immigrant Muslim communities. In Iran cousins are preferred, but here in America, many marry non-Iranian Muslims and other Americans. Parents, however, still pay a great deal of attention to marriage for their children. Families seek compatible spouses and are usually intimately involved in the selection, even in secular families. Class is an important issue in marriage, as is wealth. Traditionally, an official *khastegaree* (engagement) commences after both parties agree. The dowry in Persian, *mehriyeh*, is understood as "the amount of monetary compensation that the future husband will have to pay his wife in the unfortunate case of a divorce."[27] The higher the *mehriyeh*, the higher the status symbol, though in religious families it may be symbolic rather than actual. As in all American families, women shop and shop for rings, gifts, and a wedding trousseau. Traditionally, middle-class women get a *jaheezeeyeh* or a collection of major home and kitchen appliances that will help them begin their new life. Parents of modest means begin these purchases long before their daughters are ready for marriage. Though the scale of traditional weddings has decreased, the symbolism is still present.

The Iranian wedding, like weddings all over the world, consists of the religious exchange of vows and the reception party. An imam performs the religious wedding ceremony called *aghd*. Of course, in the United States, couples obtain their civil license prior to the wedding. In a traditional ceremony

> the bride plays "hard to get" and makes the imam repeat his question three times before she will say *baleh* [yes]. Usually the women present will encourage her to resist. The bride and groom are under a white net, [with women] rubbing two pieces of sugar against each other. This causes the sugar to "snow" into the net, which symbolizes the sweetness, whiteness, and good fortune that is to follow from this wedding.[28]

The lives of Iranian women whether they live in Iran or in the United States come with expectations.

A Short Note on Women

We must discuss Iranian women since they were seen for 444 days on almost every TV in America during the hostage crisis as black-robed and oppressed.

There are, however, women who voluntarily emigrated from Iran, those who are in exile because of political activism, and those born in the United States. These lives meet in the arena of expectations. The discussion of the role and status of women in Iran, as a defining event in political debates, is worthy of attention here because of the stereotypes.

> Secularists will consider the position of women and the attitude toward sexuality that prevail in the West to be superior and worthy of adoption. Modernists will argue that while the status of women in the areas of work, education, legal position, and political participation is superior in the West today, Islam was originally an emancipatory movement that improved the situation of women in the Arab world dramatically. Purdah, child marriage, and women's disenfranchisement are classified as non-Islamic and stemming instead from local customs, while marriage laws and other Islamic rulings are taken to require reinterpretation according to the principles of Islam. In addition, focus will be put on the negative aspects of women's situation in the West. The Mujahideen platform argues that women must be freed from the "dark, reactionary oppression" of the fundamentalists and from the "capitalist conception of women as a commodity." Traditionalists will reject the comparison with the West, while fundamentalists will argue that the Islamic system is the only one that does justice to nature and morality.[29]

While the classification of political thoughts about women detailed above is accurate, how these thoughts compare to what Iranian women do in everyday life is conspicuously absent. Iranian-American women, for example, seem to be far more pragmatic in their pursuits. One researcher, Arlene Dallalfar, studied Iranian women's economy in Los Angeles.[30] She found the Iranian community in Los Angeles to be an entrepreneurial community where women's work is valued and necessary. This does not mean that these women escape those expected tasks of housekeeping or preparation of meals like most American women. For some Iranian women, the move to the United States has meant a complete change in class status and its conveniences. Many of these women have started at-home businesses that require very long working hours. Dallalfar notes that when the business becomes self-sustaining, many women rent a small space to move the enterprise out of the home. This move, however, requires substantial contact with the non-Iranian public and a need for language skills. On the other hand, though few in number, Iranian female scholars have made significant contributions to American academe and Islamic Studies. Ziba Mir-Hosseini in her text, *Islam and Gender* asserts:

> Women are central to the political and moral imagination in Muslim majority societies. Because of this centrality, the contest over women's roles in society and family legislation has often become a matter of high politics.

At times, however, the headscarf debate detracts from a second, more profound debate that has the potential for transforming Muslim thought and practice.[31]

9

Living on the Margins

Chinese and Somali American Muslims

Chinese Muslim interaction with other Muslims in America is growing, and on the West Coast, where they are the most numerous, their voices contribute to conversations on issues in community affairs. In some neighborhoods, they are the only Muslims around. According to one interviewee, "many people just think we are Chinese women with scarves on, if they see us at all."[1] A very brief overview of Islam in China and Chinese immigrants to America is useful in our exploration of some aspects of their lives here. The majority national group of Chinese is the Han, numbering in the hundreds of millions while Muslims comprise a significant minority divided among ten national groups, the largest of which is the Hui.

History

The actual numbers of Muslims in China is unknown though estimates range from fifteen to fifty million depending on which scholar you read. Scholars assert that the oldest mosque in Kwantung, China, is the first mosque built outside Medina.

> Muslim communities, with their mosques, madaaris [schools], halal butchers, and food stalls, and many other distinctive features, are found in almost every part of China.[2]

There is scholarly consensus that Islam came to China along the Silk Road in the seventh century during the Tang dynasty. Through a mixture of conversion and marriage, the native Chinese Muslim population grew at a steady pace over the centuries; their numbers were augmented by Central Asian Muslims moving to the northern and western regions in the ninth and tenth centuries.

Yet, few researchers, until relatively recently, even acknowledged their presence. According to Dru Gladney:

> The earliest Muslim communities were descended from the Arab, Persian, Central Asian, and Mongolian Muslim merchants, militia, and of-

> ficials who settled along China's southeast coast and in the northwest in large and small numbers from the seventh to the fourteenth centuries.[3]

Islam in China grew through intermarriage, adoption, and further migrations prior to 1784 when the Qing government outlawed conversion to Islam. The majority of Chinese Muslims who are either Chinese-speaking Hui or Uighar (Central Asian) are Sunni. The entry of Islam into China's Buddhist, Taoist, Confucian landscape required that Chinese Muslims build enclaves, separated from, yet interacting with, the larger Chinese population. Each Muslim village had one *masjid* and a rotating *ahong* (imam), who moved along every three years. Senior elders in each village formed the governing council. China's landscape became dotted with Muslim villages that contained no Han citizens and Han villages with no Hui. This physical separation enabled Muslims to nurture their religion and its different cultural, worship, and dietary preferences.

Despite internal disputes, Chinese Muslim identity is firm. From early dynasties, Islam was labeled "Pure and True Faith" (Qing Zhen Jiao)—the Correct Religion. The Chinese characters for pure and true are found everywhere Hui are living.

> In the seventeenth-century work Qing Zhen Jiao Shuo (of the Pure and True Religion), Liu Sanxiu, father of the famous Ming-dynasty Islamic scholar Liu Zhi, wrote that Islam comprises 3 elements: "The purity and truth of Allah, religion, and humankind" (zhu de qing zhen, jiao de qing zhen he ren de qing zhen). Ma Fuchu (1794–1874), the Yunan Hui scholar, defined qing zhen in terms of Confucian ideals when he wrote: "to deny oneself is pure, to restore propriety is true.[4]

Chinese Muslims since their beginnings have struggled with Islamic notions of moral purity and ritual cleanliness in a society that is both polytheistic and pork-loving. The concept of *qing zhen* is so central to Chinese Muslim religious concerns that the *shahada* is known in Chinese as the *Qing Zhen Yan*.

Living as Chinese also dictated a reworking of folktales to include Islam. Muslim folktales are a unique blend of Islamic and Buddhist sensibilities with Confucian practicality and Taoist notions of ying and yang. A good example of this blending is found in Chinese mythological interpretations of the Islamic creation story, of which there are three.

> According to the first two versions, the angelic Adam and Eve were expelled from heavens as punishment for sin. And by contrast, the third version rather concretely narrates the creation of Adam from the five colors of earth. This earthward orientation links up nicely with other Near Eastern traditions, as well as with traditional Chinese Panku mythology.[5]

Interestingly, in the first two versions, atonement for the "sin" of eating becomes Qur'anic recitation and five times daily prayer, all leading to sexual ability. Though there is little Qur'anic evidence for the particulars of any of the versions, the Islamic and Chinese fusion is evident. Perhaps the organization of thought underlying these mythological formations can be found in Confucianism, Buddhism, and/or Taoism. Taoism is bound up with the necessities of the everyday life, especially rituals. Believers attempt to come to terms in this life with the process of the universe—the alternations of the yin and yang. Confucianism certainly lends some of its thought to these and other tales. Confucius was concerned with the principles of order and harmony in society so that justice and happiness would prevail. Propriety (*Li*), Reciprocity (*Li As Shu*), and Cooperation in securing the general good (*Ren*) are obviously shared traits with the Qur'anic assertions. Whatever the influences, Chinese Muslim mythology and folktales are rich in parables and textures, providing essential grounding in both their Chinese and Muslim heritages.

In many of the tales that address family matters, the emphasis is on good treatment of parents. Children learn the importance of parental wisdom and the need for compassion and loyalty. Young married couples are taught universal lessons about remembering their parents' needs. In one story a couple has four sons, who through their parents' frugality, grow up and make good marriages. The sons and their wives live their lives forgetting to provide food or clothing for their parents. Starving and sick, the parents set out to get their attention by pretending to wrap up their precious belongings, which are actually just stones, in colorful paper and put them in a chest they then lock.

Doing this several evenings in a row in front of their window so that someone notices, word is passed through the village about their activities and eventually gets to their sons. The sons, suspecting some unknown treasures, begin to vie for their parents' attention with food and clothing and rotations of caring for them. Having been left so long without care, the elderly parents soon die, and the sons pay for elaborate funerals. Immediately after the last funeral they rush to open the chest, fully prepared to discover treasures, find stones, and finally realize their series of faults.

While the collections of proverbs and tales from the various regions certainly reflect the ideals of Chinese Muslims, they are also examples of synchrony between the religious and philosophical norms with Hui at the center. This large minority community is very much in control of its place both in the Muslim and Chinese worlds. To remember dynasties—friendly, neutral, and hostile to Islam—Chinese Muslims preserved various encounters in tales. One of these tales focuses on the cruelty of Han Chinese during the Qing dynasty through a story of twin Hui boys, too poor to go to school, learning how to read and write by standing outside the school overhearing lessons. The headmaster discovers them and outrageously insults them resulting in their commission of suicide. The young men are resurrected and get the best scores on the imperial exams—a feat that ensures a salary for life. Another story tells of an ignorant supervisor who decides that because Hui congregate in the mosque, they must be plotting rebellion against the Imperial Court. He presents his fabricated evidence to the court expecting a promotion only to find out that the court already knows about Hui and their Islamic practices. This supervisory official is castigated for his fraud and ignorance as the Hui were not known for rebellion.

Chinese Muslims were engaged with the officials of two very powerful dynasties, the Ming and the Qing, for over five hundred years. Concurrently, Europe was achieving its Renaissance, Columbus was trying to find his way, Aztecs were struggling to survive genocide, the trans-Atlantic slave trade was in full throttle, Machiavelli was writing *The Prince,* and King Henry VIII was founding the Church of England. Not only did Chinese Muslims survive, they managed to insert themselves into non-Muslim Chinese folklore and the religious landscape permanently.

Zheng He (1371–1433) became the first Chinese Muslim admiral and arguably China's most famous navigator. A world traveler to East Africa, Makkah (Arabia), the Persian Gulf, and throughout the Indian Ocean, he earned his place in Chinese history. He came to this position as a young man who had assisted a Chinese prince destined to be an emperor of the Ming dynasty. How his name became intertwined with Chinese folklore is the "great stuff" of history. Zheng He (who was born Ma He) made his way into immortality in Chinese traditional folklore along with a Marshall Ma, which was the name of a Buddhist monk. As the story goes, the patron god of horses in China is named Ma. In traditional Chinese folklore the monk provided the name, and Taoists made him a god of fire—a cosmic configuration that can be manipulated, that is influenced. Tantric Buddhism influenced his representation as an exceptionally flexible but most often three-headed, six-armed, blue entity.

Ma became the name of a stellar constellation eventually associated with one particular star, which became the focus of Chinese who kept horses. Finally, shortly after Admiral Ma's time, Ma emerged as a Muslim, became a common Muslim surname, and so the patron god of horses in China is a Muslim named Ma. Because he is understood to be a patron god, Muslims themselves take the name but have nothing to do with the shrine where he is worshipped. Ma's non-Muslim patrons ironically offer him mutton or beef, but never pork. Zheng He died in the tenth year of the reign of the Ming emperor Xuande and was buried in the southern outskirts of Nanjing. Inscribed on the top of his Ming-style tomb are the Arabic words, "Allahu Akbar (God is Great)."[6]

Chinese Muslim Women

One other aspect of Chinese Muslim history and contemporary life is also an extraordinary example of synchrony—Chinese Muslim women's *masajid.*

> In order for Muslim women to define and defend their interest, in order to learn to take advantage of diverse traditions of innovative religious praxis, they must first understand the cultural diversification to which Islamic thought and institutions have been exposed.[7]

Chinese Muslim women, like other Chinese women, are heirs to the patriarchal world of Confucianism. With the Tao (Dao) understood as the "ultimate ordering principle in the world"—the road or path, the charting of stars and thus, the celestial patterns, there came the notions of yin and yang to explain the repeated behaviors. *Yin* means "covered by clouds," thus, dark, hidden, secret, and so forth, while *yang* refers to something bright and shiny, thus, open and warm. These two opposites are understood as the basis of things, even sexuality. In the gender/sexual realm, males are yang—open, active, and aggressive; while females are yin—hidden, passive, and yielding. The system is good because it is the "Way of Heaven" and consequently the proper ordering of the world. Chinese Muslims adhere to these understandings but use the harmonizing lens of Islam to yield a different outcome.

Three renowned Chinese Muslim scholars Wang Daiyn (1584–1670), Ma Zhu (1640–1711) and Liu Zhi (1655–1745), of the Ming and Qing dynasties are said to have provided the framework for "the construct of the ideal Muslim woman in the Islamic diaspora in Central China." Using both Taoist (Daoist) and Confucian ethical systems but applying an Islamic lens, they all tackled the status of women, giving them a freedom regarding spirituality and learning unmatched anywhere in the world, especially the Muslim world. All three scholars accept the notions and the implications of yin and yang. Women, though subservient in everything domestic, are not inferior in potential spiritually or in Islamic learning. They must attempt to pursue Islamic education to avoid going to hell with those men who are weak and cast aside their natural ability to excel. This framework laid a firm foundation for women's schools, women's *masajid* attached to men's *masajid* (run by men), and independent women's *masajid.*

Muslim lifestyles adjusted to "Confucian standards" but "religion was shaped by the principles of Islam."

> Qing Dynasty scholars situated Chinese Muslim women in worldly and religious spheres. In secular life, women were left almost no space for development beyond the domestic courtyard. However, they were encouraged to develop in religious life.[8]

Thus, Chinese Muslims have the only female religious culture that centers on "mosques specifically built for Muslim women to perform religious ablutions, participate in worship, acquire some basic knowledge concerning precepts and rites, and to learn about female physiology under the guidance of a *nu ahong* (female religious leader, women's mosque)."[9] During the sixteenth and seventeenth centuries formal Islamic religious education and an Islamic school for women was established. Women's *masajid* run by *nu ahong* were founded during the reign of Jiaqing (1796–1820).

Apparently, during the "era of consolidation" in China in the early seventeenth century, women's roles were confined to the home. Yet the social position of Muslims was in decline, and knowledge of Islam was considered endangered. It did not take much thought to recognize an ally in the strategies to preserve the integrity of the Muslim community—women. Jaschok and Jingjun also assert:

> We have no knowledge of the exact number of prestigious *nu junshi* (female scholars of senior rank), but we can be sure that over five hundred years ago (in the late fifteenth century), respectable *nu junshi* existed, and women's talents and roles were acknowledged and approved by Muslims.[10]

Education for women consists of several tiers. Primary education is the same for men and women and includes basic religious courses, basic Arabic language, Islamic history, Qur'anic study, and the basics of Islamic practice. Advanced students also studied Persian to add to their knowledge of Chinese and Arabic. Needless to say, the outcome of the emphasis provided by the framework of scholars provided women with an opportunity that remains today. Also of great interest is the fact that this model has not been duplicated even by Muslim women in Western societies. Though Islam in China is definitely Chinese, Muslims have not changed the religion; rather they have infused the Islamic ethical system with recognizable aspects of Chinese culture, thereby dismissing notions that they are something other than Chinese.

> As far as modern Chinese Muslims are concerned, Islamic Law, a meticulously wrought system defining extensive obligations based on religious ethics, cannot constitute the sole normative source of social conduct. In China's vast and long history, the Islamic laws have collided, fused and been assimilated with traditional Chinese cultural norms and post-Confucian secular changes and re-merging traditions.[11]

Yet, despite a long history of women's achievement in the religious realm, Chinese Muslim women, as do all Muslim women, have to dialogue in spirit if not in person with the definition of Muslim women conveyed by Arab women. One aspect of the construct surrounding Arab women besides their lack of achievement in the realm of spirituality is the notion of purity, most often symbolized by veils and *jalaba* (cloaks). That the notion of purity has become related to "women's quest for spiritual equality" in the Arab world is almost ludicrous in the world of Chinese Muslim women who have inherited a vehicle for achievement. Nevertheless, Chinese Muslims are engaged in the age-old battles surrounding the particular Arab construct of women and their roles, albeit from a different starting point.

Chinese Muslim voices and participation (female and male) on matters of specific concern to their ethnic-religious identity are quite robust. The events of the 1989 democratic movement in China, called the "Salman Rusdie in China" protest, was a nationwide demonstration of Muslims that took place at the peak of the 1989 "Democracy Movement" in China.[12] In 1989, led by Muslim students, a protest was organized to challenge the content of *Sexual Customs* (*Xing fengsui*). The protesters asserted that the authors denigrated Islam just "like the *Satanic Verses*."

> The book was an innocuous description of the history of sexuality around the world, which guaranteed it a strong market in China where few official books address the subject. Muslims in China would normally pay little attention to such popular literature. They were violently incensed, however, by sections of the book dealing with Islam that compared minarets to phalli, Muslim tombs and domes to the mound of "Venus,"and the Meccan pilgrimage to orgies, which were an excuse, the book claimed, for homosexual relations and sodomy, with camels, no less.[13]

Chinese officials permitted the protests, banned the book, burned over ninety-five thousand copies in the main square of Lanzhou, fired the editors, required the authors to make a public apology, and closed publication houses. Though few in the West ever heard, every detail was covered in the world's media. Lest the reader think that everything is fine for Muslims in China, there is a long history of antagonisms based primarily on the fact that Islam is a foreign religion. This incident is one of the more famous in a long list of issues surrounding publications denigrating Islam and its practices in the twentieth century alone.

Immigration to the United States

The second half of the nineteenth century proved an extremely difficult time for China. Five of her ports were under the control of foreign powers as a result of the Chinese government's losing efforts to keep British opium, grown in India, out of China. The resultant unrestricted trade under Western nations severely weakened the economy causing both social disintegration and near political collapse.[14] Domestic rebellions such as the Christian-influenced Taiping Rebellion (1850–1864) for religious reform resulted in the deaths of over twenty million people and the destruction of large areas of profitable land.

These internal devastations, along with the need of colonial powers for cheap labor, propelled thousands of Chinese to the West for work and opportunity. Many Chinese were recruited under a credit-ticket system whereby the costs of passage were to be repaid from future labor—indentured servitude.

Chinese Americans enjoy, with Germans and Irish Americans, the status of belonging to the group of earliest immigrants. They were in America much earlier than any of the southern and eastern Europeans. However, despite early arrival and an exceptionally strong work ethic, the Chinese experienced one of the most unique and painful experiences of all immigrant groups. Exclusion and miscegenation laws kept them isolated in urban ghettos under the title "alien." There was no expectation or desire that they become American. Historians assert that most of the half million early Chinese immigrants who came between 1850 and 1900 came from an area in southern China around Canton.

The need for Chinese labor encouraged the 1868 Burlingame Treaty with China, which for a few decades provided for unlimited immigration to the United States. After the abolition of African slavery, Chinese indentured servitude was highly sought, especially in the western regions of the United States. The Chinese Exclusion Act of 1882 ushered in a new era for Chinese immigrants—restricted entry for the next five decades. Though the act was repealed in 1943, Chinese found themselves in a quota system until the passage of the Civil Rights Act of 1964. They were then able to take advantage of federally funded programs to establish businesses and pursue higher education.

Chinese Americans

As with many religiously plural nations and according to policy, U.S. Immigration Services does not list Chinese immigrants by religion. Thus we would be only guessing as to how many Chinese immigrants and their descendents are Muslim. Given this fact, we can explore what is actually known of the Chinese in the United States.

> There are many theories and much evidence to support the contention that some of the people on hand to greet Columbus were descendents of adventurers or shipwrecked seamen from the ancient Celestial Empire called China.[15]

Records show the first Chinese immigrants came in 1847; it was not until the cry of gold went up in California that the Chinese arrived in large numbers.[16] By 1851 it was estimated that twenty-five thousand Chinese were living in California. As with many non-European immigrants, men came first. By the 1880s, 75 percent of all farmhands in California were Chinese. This number may be exaggerated because we also know of large numbers of South Asians working on the farms in California during the same time. Nevertheless, history equally extols Chinese laborers as the main labor pool in building the intercontinental railroad and as a despised people who were "murdered, lynched, deported, or left in the wilderness to die." Further complicating our study is the fact that during almost eight years of exclusion, "Chinese immigrants were not permitted to become citizens no matter how long they had lived here."[17] So, there are few references to them in citizenship records. Until 1970 the census provided socioeconomic statistics for only three racial categories: black, white, and other—also complicating research.

Chinese Americans live predominantly in California, New York, Hawaii, Massachusetts, and Illinois. Among them are Chinese Muslims. In each of these states the sign "Pure and True" hangs over stores and restaurants. In Los Angeles about three hundred Chinese Muslims regularly gather to "talk about religious tenets, social values, and their Chinese identities."[18] At the heart of many discussions across the country among Chinese Muslims is the relationship between the American and Chinese governments. Chinese Muslims are very much aware of their over one-hundred-thirty-year problematic diaspora in the United States and tend to be a self-contained community with little intermingling with other Muslims except on major holidays.[19]

Somali Americans

> There are no rules here! Everything is freedom! What does freedom mean? Freedom to be gay or take drugs or whatever?![20]

"What/Who is your clan?" The answer to this question both in Somalia and in the United States determines your status and quality of life. Somalia is located on the Horn of Africa, smaller than the state of Texas, a hot, dry land all year round. According to all encyclopedias, the word *Somali* is derived from two words that roughly mean, "milk to self." Fleeing civil war that formally began in 1990 and disintegrated into clan warfare, Somali refugees have found themselves in considerable numbers in Midwestern U.S. states such as Minnesota and Ohio. Representative of one of the longest Islamic histories on the continent of Africa, Somalis experienced considerable trauma as a result of European imperialism and almost a decade of civil war. Europeans divided up the region into colonies; Somalia was not a state until the end of the nineteenth century. The Italians controlled the southern area of Somalia until 1943, while northern Somalia was controlled by the British until 1960. Unification of the regions took place with independence in 1960.

Somalis are almost all Sunni Muslims who live in a system of patriarchal clans.

> By calculating descent along paternal lines, every Somali can position him or herself in one particular clan. The clan, or a subgroup of it, is what has traditionally served as a social security system, judicial system and unit of solidarity in times of warfare.[21]

Islam came to the state called Somalia in the seventh century, and regardless of clan affiliation, almost all Somalis strongly identify as Muslims. The history of Islam in the country is mostly oral until 1972 when there was the development of an official orthography and subsequent record keeping. But the status of clans, along with the identity and security they provide, are the basis of life. Northern pastoral clans, who consider themselves a nobility of sorts with Arab ancestry, are culturally different from the southern, more racially mixed clans, who previously were slaves or clients. Both northerners and southerners have combined traditions of ancestor worship, traditional knowledge, and magic into their Islamic practices. Each group has Islamic movements whose aim is to rid themselves of Sufism, saints, and shrines.

As in many parts of the Muslim world, tradition remains in the Islamic practice and is often engaged by Sufism. Men and women who lead exemplary religious lives often wind up as saints and are thought to have some special contact with God and, thus, some particular ability to act as mediators between God and humans. Sufism, in addition to its overall appeal to the spiritual side of any believer, particularly appeals to the disenfranchised. When many southern Somalis were manumitted from slavery in the mid 1920s, Sufis were able to establish settlements that served in the twentieth century as safe havens. But Sufism also spread throughout the society, cementing itself as a part of Somali Islam but providing fertile ground for attacks from Saudi-influenced "pure" Islam. One explicit example, as always, is observable in the dress of women.

> Traditionally Somali women have never worn veils, but revealed both arms and shoulders wearing their colorful traditional dress—guntiino. However, from the late 1980s, women's dress code began to change with the introduction of Saudi-inspired attires, often supplemented by a veil. This dress, known in Somalia as shuko, covers the entire body with the exception of the feet and hands.[22]

These movements also brought additional burdens to women. Modern "returns to a pure Islam" have also translated into more clothing and limitations on the freedom of movement for Muslim women. One corollary is the prevention of education.

While in Somalia the function of the clan is unambiguous as it regulates everyday life, in America clan affiliation is under serious scrutiny as members participate in a different way of life. In Somalia, clan members memorize their genealogy to situate relationships and declare status. In the United States neighbors are more apt to want to know who you are now. As mentioned earlier, family in America may include members who are not blood relations. Nevertheless, Somali identity is still reckoned in this way of making clans a transportable community in the United States. As more Somalis make their way to the United States, clan affiliation becomes the network for settling in and determines the ease or dis-ease of the diaspora.

Somalis in the United States

In the United States, Somalis number between thirty thousand and forty thousand with approximately fifteen to seventeen thousand living in Minnesota and almost the same number in Ohio. The first Somali immigrants came truly as immigrants, not refugees of civil war, in the 1920s. With a diaspora population of approximately one million, only a few have sought to make the United States a new home. The difficulties in settling in are mostly the same as those we encountered with other Muslim immigrants. The customs of the culture are also similar to many others in the Muslim world.

Arranged marriages are quite common between members of the same clan whether in Milwaukee or Mogadishu. Customary family obligations are still enforced too. The most fortunate assist the least fortunate and the elders, with the father's family members given the most consideration. Children, like elsewhere in the Muslim world, keep their family name and status of their family's clan. The demands of the clan traveled easily across the ocean.

> Somali refugees in Minnesota have sent at least $15 million to East Africa. Most of the money—sent by individuals in the chunks of $100 to $600 a month—is humanitarian aid for people caught in the violence of a country ruled by warring clans, according to interviews with Somalis in the Twin Cities area.[23]

One ongoing tension in the diaspora centers on whether or not sending money back to Somalia is only fueling the clan war rather than helping families out of poverty. In the segregated communities in the United States, many feel pressured to contribute because if they don't contribute then they will be ostracized. For many, contributions of more than fifty dollars a month are difficult because of problems with employment and rising living expenses.

> My family is just fed up. There are nine of us and my father just lost his fourth job. We have been in the United States for six years and it has been difficult. Learning English, getting jobs, clothing expenses, hospital bills, everything costs money. We don't know where the money goes since it is a lot of money in Somalia. They think because we live in America we are rich.[24]

Somali Muslims living in Minnesota have had to truly embrace their racial brethren—African Americans. On Minnesota public radio on February 5, 2002, Brandt Williams covered the *We Win Institute*. This institute endeavors to "help African American children to excel in school and in life, by using lessons steeped in the traditions of African cultures."[25] It also connects Somali and African American students. The two cultures clash culturally, one with a European cultural background and the other with an African one. There is no dating across cultures; not necessarily because of ethnocentricity but because Somali girls do not date. After September 11, 2001, most Somalis in the area felt that African Americans were very supportive of their plight.

Even prior to September 11, as early as 1997 as a matter of fact, Somalis were deported back to Somalia to the same cities they fled even though they were in the United States legally. Many had lived in the United States for years with little facility in the Somali language. Not until the beginning of 2003 did a judge finally declare these deportations illegal even though the United States has not recognized a government in Somalia since 1991. Recently the U.S. government has decided to grant entry to twelve thousand Somali Bantu refugees, the other portion of the clan fights in Somalia. Fortunately for the moment, none are resettling in Minnesota, though areas close by, such as Chicago, Milwaukee, and Sioux Falls, South Dakota are on the list. Tensions between the old and new refugees are high. Nevertheless, the need to be around familiar countrymen may win out in the end, only time will tell.

Somali, like Chinese Muslims, are just beginning to make themselves known as potential leaders in the general Muslim community. They are increasing their presence at conventions, seminars, and leadership conferences.

10

Global Islam in America

The Mix and the Challenges

The initial conquests by Arab armies, according to historians, did not first bring the religion of Islam to the conquered. They first stabilized their military and political hold over soon to be "new" Muslims. They then followed with the deployment of men learned in the Qur'an and with knowledge of the Prophet's (pbuh) life. *Mawali* (converts), however, had little access to participation in the Arabian center of Islam and had to embellish factual accounts and genealogies to connect themselves. At the beginning of Islam, *Arab* was not a cultural entity as it described the many tribes inhabiting a geographical space. Additionally, some peoples were able to become Arab, though many initially resisted Arabization as a threat to their cultural identity. Historians have also debated which came first, Arabization or Islamization. Interestingly, there is little literature on the boundary created, when Arabization closed as a culturally accessible category, until very recently. Perhaps this issue was just not the focus of historical researches because of the Arabization versus Islamization debates. Many peoples of the Maghrib, for example, became clients of Arab tribes not only to claim portions of the booty of conquests but also to make connections to power in the absence of familial connections.

> There is also a specifically Islamic paradigm for such "communal conversion" in the "conversion-to-community" of the first century of Islam's spread, whereby adoption of the "religion of Islam" amounted to joining the "community" not of Muslims, but of Arabs, specifically in acquiring "client" status in affiliation with a particular Arab tribe.[1]

For those living outside the constructed "Arab realm," a variety of mechanisms arose to cement a relationship as new Muslims sought to connect with Arabs. New Muslims made links with Islamized genealogies, or "seeded" themselves into stories of the travels of the Prophet's (pbuh) companions, or even more creatively, placed converts in their culture as one of the Prophet's (pbuh) interlocutors during his mi'raj.[2] As history has shown, many of these constructions became accepted as fact and enlarged the families of the prophet Muhammad (pbuh) and his companions considerably.[3] Family names became associated and privileges and status quickly became the reward. Members of these families also made a point of excelling in Qur'anic studies and Islamic sciences. But what counted most was the degree of Islamic authenticity and legitimacy assigned to these families. Issues of authenticity and legitimacy have clouded almost every aspect of Islamic history and are again determining the priorities for immigrant Muslim life in America. Though Arabs have in recent years tried to deflect the focus on their influence by truthfully asserting their small numbers in Islam, they have never given over the authority brought by speaking Arabic.

Though there was a multiplicity of competing claims for leadership of an enormously knowledge-wealthy and materially rich world, there wasn't an expectation of "sameness." Muslims in different cultures were expected to be different. This aspect of Islam is best seen in hajj (pilgrimage to Mecca). An observer could assert that the diversity was an attractive aspect of the Muslim community. Debates, however, always raged over additions to or deviations from core, accepted Qur'anic interpretations rather than specific cultural practices. The problems with deviant cultural practices, on the other hand, have always been the objects of reform movements. The divisions between Sunni and Shi'a multiplied as communities battled for authority and, ultimately, leadership. Still, Arab thought controlled everything. Other Muslims were bound to incorporate Arab models, respond to them, or reject them on an ongoing basis.

All civilizations, history teaches us, rise and fall due mostly to their own complacency, greed, and/or internal corruption. Every fallen civilization also spends time in denial of its role in its own demise. Blame for cultural demise is usually placed on conspiracies involving outside forces as well as those inside the culture. The agenda of those forces is always described in binary terms—either fighting evil or supporting good. Arab Muslims have blamed the demise of Muslim civilization on everything from the imperialisms of the West to their cultures' straying from Islamic ideals. Arab Muslims have also claimed that they have been limited in their rejection of corrupt Muslim leadership by the interventions of Western forces. Yet Muslim legalists paved the way for corrupt leadership by asserting that leadership is a necessity even if it is corrupt, because no leadership means chaos.[4]

> . . . as long as Muslim jurists could be recognized as the guardians of religious law, they were willing to ignore issues concerning political justice and even to lend support to unjust rulers.[5]

> . . . correlative with this development was an insistence by the jurists on the idea of obedience to those in authority, and that disorder was worse than injustice.[6]

This state of affairs has crippled Muslims for centuries. Now Muslims have emerged in the philosophically liberal West. Here there are new tools of thought and knowledge available to them. Now they have the means to assist the Muslim world in its struggle to emerge from its morass. The issues of authenticity and legitimacy, nevertheless, remain unresolved, especially given the modern transnational quality of Muslim life.

The historical scenario has been that Arab Muslims export Islam to the world and that they take creature comforts from the world. The Muslim world, however, is in such a state of "backwardness" that it is questionable if they are willing or able to receive advice from Muslims living and thriving outside of that world. Such advice would provide information about different methods of interpretation and analysis necessary for thriving in the modern world. The achievement of a knowledge-exchange scenario would, of course, require the relinquishing of some authority. The habits of past ways are entrenched, however, and in the United States the battle for the definition of Islam is a vicious internal war between indigenous and immigrant American Muslims. In many ways this war is about the sanctity of traditions in a modern world. For Muslims in the West, success will be measured by the degree to which they resolve internal wars. Critical to that outcome is the ability of each of the contenders to hold to a course that is pragmatic, given to letting go of that which is no longer culturally viable.

While undoubtedly there has been a preponderance of Arab thought controlling Islamic understandings and depictions, other Muslim cultures have also understood themselves as representatives of Islam in the world. These include Muslims of many ethnic groups, but primarily Arabs and South Asians have formed what could be considered to be one of the world's largest diasporas. Both have taken their version of Islam to South Africa, East Africa, South America, and Australia. South Asians have sought to use their considerable financial resources to lend authenticity and authority. In places in the world where there are few or no Arabs, other Muslims can claim authority. At the other end, Chinese Muslims have not chosen to pursue opportunities in non-Muslim lands, thus, little is known of their Islamic practice.[7] Yet, all Muslim communities' authority defers to Arab preeminence.

Issues of Legitimacy

Is there any one group that has the right to define Islam in America? Among seemingly endless challenges to Muslim Americans is the challenge of an Islamic intellectual tradition that has become distorted, disconnected, and irrelevant. As stated earlier, the intellectual traditions of the *Ummah* were long ago captured and sometimes held hostage by the intellectual tradition of the Arab world. Modern Arab thought has further been challenged by its interaction with Western Europe, its incipient responses to Western hegemony, and by the social and political affects of Wahhabism and Salafism. But the beginnings of many of the problems are much older.

Soon after the death of the Prophet (pbuh), Muslim fragmentation began. On one hand, the spread of culturally situated Islam across the world continued at the same time Muslims in the early community returned to their tribalisms. The Quraysh tribe, to which the prophet of Islam belonged and those who could claim early membership, became special persons—*siddiq*. Consensus even of the learned (the Sunni model) in choosing leadership was truncated before it began as could be seen in deciding succession. The old traditions of leadership emanating from the tribe along with patriarchy again became the norm. Muslim women, even the *sahabah* (companions of the Prophet [pbuh]), experienced attempts to suppress their voices, though that was in contradiction to the Prophet's (pbuh) practices. Dissent became heretical and remained so well into the twenty-first century. Spurious *Hadith* on the inferiority of women, their inherently evil presence, absorbed from Christianity and the patriarchy of polytheism, were firmly planted alongside *sahih* (authentic) *Hadith* contradicting them. Bilal ibn Rabah was the first muezzin (person who calls community to prayer five times daily) and an African slave who was freed during the advent of Islam. His was a model experience. However, after the Prophet's (pbuh) death, Qur'anic exhortations to free slaves were ignored. What could be seen in these incidents, having dangerous consequences for the flowering of a strong intellectual tradition, is the distortion of the idea of consensus. Consensus, broad unanimity among the believers, on issues of governance diminished until it became the agreement of only a very few of an elite class. Professor Abu El-Fadl rightly asserts that

> the idea conveyed and constantly reinforced by one's teachers is that Islam rejects elitism and emphasizes that truth is equally accessible to all Muslims regardless of race, class or gender. At the same time that one encounters the traditions and doctrines mentioned above, he also encounters a very different trend stressing the need for unity, uniformity, clarity and simplicity. Often, the very same teachers who lectured on the doctrines of accessibility, egalitarianism, and diversity would lecture endlessly about the dangers of corrupt innovations (bida), fitan (sen-fitnah, discord or dividedness) and the evils of intellectualism and theological disputations (ilm al-kalam).[8]

He goes on to remind researchers that there are "numerous methodological problems with the doctrine of consensus" as now understood. How does one verify a consensus, and whose consensus counts? Does the consensus of one generation bind subsequent generations? Muslims distorted the essential meaning of consensus to mean "to emphasize clarity, simplicity and unity." In other words, they took the product as primary over the process. As a result the diversity of opinions on issues has been lost. Correctness of thought has been reduced to the property of a few privileged persons and their ideas. The dynamism of debate and disputation is long forgotten and dissension is *bida* (innovation) and un-Islamic rather than a part of a process leading to consensus. This lack of broad agreement and the formation of a small elite masked the wide range of available thought.

Traditionally Muslims in each culture are introduced to a selected range of Arabic thought. Though the literature seemingly is both vast and diverse, actually it usually represents two sides of the same thought, Arab responses to colonialism and neocolonialism. Those responses are limited in creativity and in scope. Of importance is the fact that those responses were exported to the United States ex cathedra unbounded in relevancy by time or circumstance. For example, Egyptian Muslims' adoption of those responses via the writings of Hasan Al-Banna and Sayyid Qutb blocked their achievement of a more relevant response to colonialism.[9] Another example is Mawlana Maududi's treatise on Muslim women. He asserts that women should stay in their homes, be fully cloaked when they do move about in public, and that they should not attend either funerals or burials.[10] Again, these understandings were brought to America as the prescription for indigenous Muslim women.

The complete absence of communication between various Muslim cultures prevents the exchange of both knowledge and experience. Each culture only knows its own philosophies, scientists, and colonial experiences. Those who experienced one type of colonization have not consulted others with different experiences. All have been left to fend for themselves with only Arab thought being disseminated as the universal Muslim voice. Ironically, Arabs are the first to describe the expanse of an *ummah* they know little about on an intimate basis and the last to search its knowledge bank for solutions. Here in the United States, the potential of the *ummah* to be an *ummah* is great but the fact that the Arab and now South Asian struggle for control of it portends future obstacles.

For many immigrant imams and their followers, non-Muslims are "disbelievers" and not fit for associating with other than at school or work and most recently in order to get ahead in politics. These notions are at the center of the Islam brought by many immigrant imams to American *mawali*. African American Sunni Muslims were given the same information about Islam as their coreligionists around the world—a salafi/wahhabist voice rose in critique of past European incursions in the Muslim world. Because this philosophy has also intertwined itself in most modern Islamic thought, it is hard for new Muslims to discern. Dressing and naming habits followed the most influential ethnic community. The only African American Muslims who escaped the indoctrination were those who also added nationalist philosophies to their Islamic understanding such as Malcolm X. When Malcolm X was alive, and for a significant time after his death, immigrant Muslims asserted that he was not really Muslim, with the same attitude held toward Muhammad Ali until very recently.

Even after September 11, 2001, many immigrant Muslim leaders kept their focus on control of the community. Little changed regarding what issues were addressed even though the fears of a besieged community were palpable. Almost every imam exulted when his picture made the newspaper or after being interviewed on TV. Typically, their representations of Islam wavered between "Muslims are peaceful" and "true Muslims are non-violent" to diatribes against U.S. backing of Israel against Palestinians. There was little evidence of the application of knowledge and reflection and no hint of voices emergent from deliberative consensus regarding the critical issues and concerns about which the media sought them out.

The Status of Global Islam at the Beginning of the Twenty-First Century

In this, the beginning of the twenty-first century, Muslims are firmly bound in anachronisms and masks. Muslims have lived transnationally for centuries in contact with their root society but also planted (though not firmly) in the new society. One aspect of modern transnationality is the increasing sets of problems it poses for nation states. Here an analogy with plants and their roots is perhaps the best example of one problem. Roots of plants form systems. The main root divides as it grows down into branches called lateral roots. These further divide to form a network that anchors the plant in the ground. New growth takes place at the ends of the smallest roots in the network. It is here that the nutrients are absorbed and then channeled back to the main root, enabling the plant to grow. Transnationals are those smallest roots. They absorb technology, goods for trade, and other cultural artifacts to nurture the home culture. One result is the enrichment of the home (root) culture and the transfer of technologies and other cultural artifacts out of the new society.[11] There is really little necessity for the transnational to change ways or means of operating as they are largely successful. The rising antagonists are the demands of some Western states for both reciprocity and civic participation along with excising themselves of transnationals altogether.

As Muslims in the West assert Qur'anic messages of justice, equality, and modest living, the realities of their racism, difficulties living in relatively open, pluralistic societies, and difficulties in getting along with each other, reveal massive contradictions. The almost absolute absence of justice, gender and class equity, along with the extremely poor living conditions among the masses in most Muslim societies make Muslims in the West appear disingenuous when claiming adherence to Qur'anic norms. Even though jurists held a virtual vise-grip on every aspect of life in Muslim societies for centuries, in modern times when governments converted their status from independent to dependent on the salaries given them, legitimate religious authority became a thing of the past. Authority could be (is) seized by anyone and has become the center of the internal struggle. One aspect of the struggle over authority is the emergence of Salafism and Wahhabism as authoritative, as both provide that decentralization of authority.

One set of issues surrounding Salafism and Wahhabism are very much in the category of which came first—the chicken or the egg. *Salaf*, meaning predecessors, refers to the model of the Prophet's (pbuh) community and the first three generations as the best Muslim communities to emulate in Muslim life. Salafi is a movement that locates religious authority and legitimacy in the models of those generations through an emphasis on the law. This is not a new position, rather one that various Muslim communities have taken over the centuries. Its impulse has arisen whenever Muslim leadership or the general community seems to stray from the middle path in social and/or political affairs as indicated by chaos or saint-worship. It has, by virtue of the movements of Muslims around the world, an insistent transnational quality.

Wahhabism on the other hand is directly associated with modern Islamic history in Arabia and with the person of Muhammad Ibn al-Wahhab who died in 1792. This movement arose as a reform stance that was opposed to Sufism and its practices of worshiping saints and enshrining tombs. Ibn al-Wahhab also pushed for the words of the Qur'an to be understood literally, making it necessary for Muslims to deduce their duties and obligations without the need of the authority of the recognized schools of legal thought. Wahhabism, by virtue of the propagation methods of its adherents also has an insistent transnational quality. Ironically, at the time, Ibn al-Wahhab was considered the rebel and the innovator, not a traditionalist or conservative. Also ironic is the resemblance to the Protestant Reformation.

In the twentieth century Salafism and Wahhabism combine to produce a practical basis for and revolution against persistent questionable practices in Islam. The world of Islam has periodically gone through such reforms in the same way over the same issues. The difference in the twentieth century centered on imperialisms and their aftermaths. The imperial powers' decimation of the Muslim world happened at the same time as the reform movements began. The objects of reform were the governments, the elites that supported them, and

Sufi movements in Islam, not imperialistic Europe. But with the avarice of those imperial powers and their support of corrupt regimes whose activities further exacerbated the poverty of the majority, a new adversary emerged—Western governments.

Social science literature has, for decades, suggested that there is a brain drain on the Muslim world as educated Muslims leave for opportunity and for freedom. While this is certainly true at one level, I would like to suggest that much of this movement is the normal movement of transnational families into new territories. They move, join old networks, and form new networks sending money and technology back home, aiding both sides of the battle for reform. Transnational corporations also assist both sides. They bring employment for the educated but also support the status quo so they can stay in business and profit. In doing so, they nurture the root culture but also perhaps prolong the reform process.

What is painful for many transnationals is that they are no longer under the radar as some have taken internal community reform to the world stage. Muslims throughout the world have been in an era of reform at least since the fall of the Ottoman Empire. Internal reform in societies recovering from civil war or colonialism is at least as varied as the two major forms of colonialism. Political scientists have distinguished forms of colonialism as direct and indirect rule.

> Direct rule tended to generate race-based political identities: settler and native. Indirect rule, in contrast, tended to mitigate the settler-native dialectic by fracturing the race consciousness of natives into multiple and separate ethnic consciousnesses.[12]

American Muslim immigrants have experienced both types of rule and in some cases one imperialist after the other. America's racist culture enhances both forms and simultaneously denigrates Islam and Muslims as we have seen in texts and media. The quality of transnational identities (their construction and multiplicity) make the ongoing assertions of legitimacy and authenticity necessary as there is little else, and this has been the case for at least two centuries.[13] U.S. society is one place where the possibilities for a deconstruction of historical hierarchies can take place. The transnational has met a vibrant indigenous community that does not participate in the same quality of life or the possibilities of far-flung networks but has the intelligence and faithfulness necessary to use some of the tools elaborated in the West to assist a reform of the East.

Issues surrounding authority and legitimacy are also of paramount importance in the West as the definition of Islam seems to rest firmly in the hands of non-Muslims—scholars, politicians, media, and government. The obvious result is that Islam is the only world religion in the West whose esteemed scholars are of a different faith. Currently the Bush government is encouraging Western, non-Muslim scholars to rewrite the Qur'an and its interpretations to suit Western sensibilities.[14]

The tragedies leading up to and including those of September 11, 2001, and subsequent discriminations against and detentions/deportations of Muslims forced the need for a definition of Islam. Prior to those events and increasingly since then, many "new" experts, almost all non-Muslims emerged and defined Islam as a violent, hate-filled cult, a threat to the American way of life that must be changed, and the antithesis of Christianity and Judaism.[15] Immigrant American Muslims, as individuals, were sought out to clarify Islamic tenets and to provide insight on the obvious hatred for America. Very few had even remotely reflective positions on the current events. Many were torn between a perceived need to defend Islam, a need to show love for their adopted country, and a need to maintain dignity and honor in the face of tragedy.

The most common response, mentioned earlier was "Islam just means peace." For a transnational to express patriotism in a branch community when the enemy of the patriotism is their root community is difficult if not impossible. That expressions of patriotism were demanded by the government and the people of the United States is a new experience. The uniqueness of this situation caused many transnational Muslims fear and confusion.

The Nature of the Struggle

Many immigrant Muslims came to America as transnationals without any specific plans to participate, or to engage publicly, in the society. What they found out, however, was that nonparticipation in American society is unwise since it is a society where religions compete for recognition and political clout. Rather than building alliances, forming social institutions, buying television and radio stations, or founding newspapers that dealt with American issues Muslims built *masajid*, and organizations that only served Muslims. This had been a method for penetrating new societies for at least a century. They naturally overlooked one hallmark of American society—volunteerism, which is almost unknown in the Muslim world. In fact American volunteerism is one aspect of its society that is not ethnocentric as it is the one arena of American life that is not segregated.

Though religious groups are responsible for most charitable and social service organizations, the services are rendered to all irrespective of race, gender or class. There are few if any organizations in America that do not have a charitable arm. Volunteerism, as a staple of community life, builds necessary networks across racial and social boundaries. Most transnational Muslims missed this aspect of American life and built communities that are replicas of their various homelands to include many of the social repressions from which they fled to America. While this has been a much commented upon aspect of American Muslim life, the fact that this is the life of transnational families around the world has not been explored.

American Muslim immigrants could not pretend that they, like others in history, came to a land where there were no Muslims present; yet still they persisted in creating the fiction that Islam in America began with the immigrants as they have done successfully in other places such as Central Asia or Afghanistan. What they quickly learned to do was to tolerate the presence of indigenous Muslims—especially because America was already aware of African American Islam, and immigrants could not deny this fact. African Americans had put Islam on the map of American religions with both presence and litigation, complicating a complete erasure of the past.[16] This state of affairs between the indigenous and the immigrant has added another dimension to the internal struggles of the community. Again, issues of authenticity and legitimacy are priorities.

No matter how much African American Muslims mastered the Islamic sciences or for how many generations they had existed as Muslims, they were still considered new and uncultured *mawali.* More significantly, they could not be allowed to define Islam, because they are not Arab. In an effort to prevent African Americans from defining Islam, immigrants have declared much of African American culture inappropriate for inclusion in any definition of Islam. Using both Salafism and Wahhabism as models, transnational Muslims from South Asia and the Arabic-speaking world, declared music prohibited, American clothing inappropriate, contact with Christian relatives abhorrent, and dismissed African American knowledge of America as irrelevant. They then cast Islam as unknowable for those who had been Muslim for decades. Arabic was cast as an extremely difficult language and thus, indigenous Muslims could have only limited access to Islam and thus, only limited authority. The branches of the transnational Muslim communities have finally reached the West; they have penetrated the most militarily advanced country in the world and one that has persistently invaded the sanctity of the Muslim world in recent years. Indigenous Muslims, especially African Americans, are very much aware of their history in America and the fact that almost all immigrants have directly benefited from their struggles as minorities.

African American Muslim prisoners' litigation won rights to change their names, have pork-free diets, have Muslim chaplains, have prison facilities purchase Qur'ans, thus putting Islam and Muslims in public discourse. Other African American Muslims similarly won these rights in professions such as medicine, law enforcement, and education; in public schools, and social services.

Many immigrant Muslims stepped into the benefits of these battles without any acknowledgment of them. As if there were no Muslims present, immigrant Muslims set out to build cultural organizations, *masajid,* and schools. African American Muslims were largely shut out and almost completely marginalized regarding issues of leadership and authority, setting the stage for the current debate. They have little knowledge of the lives of transnational networks even though they see them everyday.

Needless to say, numerous tensions have emerged from this state of affairs. The ethnic and cultural prejudices of transnational Muslims have obscured the principles of the Qur'an itself and thus the hopes of many indigenous Muslims that they were engaged in a religion in which they were not considered inferior. Coming from societies where both color and class are obvious markers and being extremely resistant to change, transnational Muslims of different networks are sometimes very uncomfortable with each other and definitely with blacks and Latinos. They readily usurped the role of America's Muslims, and there is much consternation in communities over their performance. Leadership roles in the Muslim world are a function of heredity, patronage, and class and this understanding was brought to America. The "clergy" are well defined in the Muslim world and though their services are paid for, no one outside of this training would ever think of usurpation.

In America many Muslims who would never have distinguished themselves for their Islamic knowledge have been able to take leadership positions. Medical doctors and engineers have assumed positions of leadership over religious organizations, schools, and the *masajid* with their financial resources, not their Islamic knowledge. Their shortcomings are only recognized when the Friday talk is from a book of Mogul lectures or about the evils of America or there is a public debate on American issues in which Muslims were not present. Transnationals have consistently imported religious leadership from "back home," and this leadership is in charge of prayers, officiate at ceremonies, and run the *masajid* to the specifications of the funders. The key to influence in the power structure however, is to move beyond voicing the needs and complaints of Muslims to action on behalf of the community. At least some endeavors must be for the larger good of the entire community. Transnational Muslims have not yet understood the wants and desires of the everyday American, and thus they remain unaffected by issues of poverty, homelessness, and unemployment, or even the responsibilities of wealth in American society. Activist citizenship is slowly becoming important. Generally speaking, the lack of civic participation is not deliberate but rather a course of action that has never been considered.

In the Muslim world professionals have little contact with the lower classes except as servants or in the service sectors, very much like here in the United

States. The disenfranchised are dismissed, ridiculed, and often left to die as there are few social organizations to assist with the needs of the majority of the population. Want ads do not exist and neither do "help wanted" signs in stores. I watched young college graduates standing on corners or sitting in cafés in Morocco with, as one young lady told me, "the hope of a possibility." In all of the communities we have explored, the children of professionals have the way paved for them. Parents believe they can buy anything from cars to grades and in the process assure the continuity of privilege much like wealthy parents in any community. They continue, naturally, to do in America what they did in their homeland. It will take time and stress to learn new ways.

One example of the difficulty in achieving effective citizenship is seen in the organization of Muslim charitable institutions. Immigrant Muslims have set up charities that are exclusive organizations. They serve the needs of their ethnic group "back home." There are no Muslim-run charitable organizations that serve everyone in a community. What they have found, especially since September 11, 2001, is that when they need social services beyond the resources of their ethnic community, such as civil rights lawyers, they have to turn to the ACLU or to other free legal clinics run by religious groups. Immigrant Muslims do not foster-parent abandoned children, Muslim or not. They however, send millions of dollars back to their homelands to build and sustain clinics, feed the hungry, and provide lodgings for orphaned children. The need to turn some of this giving back to the United States is just now becoming a thought. While we can easily say, in everything but the passport, these immigrants are still foreigners; we must also remember that many Muslim immigrants are transnationals, and we must change how we view their actions.

In our exploration of culture, we could see some religious interpretation and some of the philosophical positions. Now we need to explore the possibilities of the connections between what we learned and the current state of violence. As stated earlier internal reform in countries is generally violent. Those in power and those who serve them do not give up their privilege easily, and persistent extreme poverty, lack of control over everyday matters, along with various foreign neo-occupations entrenches resentment among the masses. The majority populations generally have nothing more to lose in the transaction of violence but can gain some sense of humanity.

> For (Frantz) Fanon, the native's violence was not life denying, but life affirming: For he knows that he is not an animal; and it is precisely when he realizes his humanity that he begins to sharpen the weapons with which he will secure its victory.[17]

Who is the adversary? As asserted previously, in those Muslim communities undergoing change, the first enemy is the leadership and then those who support that leadership from within and without. When the adversary controls almost everything about your life including how you can protest injustice and what is done about it, the choices of recourse narrow, but there are choices. Gandhi, King, and some others chose marches and quiet protests, which were met with violence from the adversary. The disenfranchised have been demonized and made nonhuman and in turn they reciprocate. "What affirmed the natives' humanity for Fanon was not that they were willing to take the settler's life, but that they were willing to risk their own: the colonized man finds his freedom in and through violence."[18] On the other side, domination and occupation were not usually accomplished nonviolently. The violence committed in occupation and subjugation is unmatched as it is done to the physical landscape, the people, and survivors' psyches. We also know that in the commission of acts of occupation and subjugation, the psyche of the imperialist is also changed for the worst. No one really wins.

Internal reform in Muslim lands has come to be played out on the world stage because of the twin forces' power to sustain the status quo. Transnational Muslims in the West are on both sides of the internal conflict. Many of them are heirs to class privilege, the same privilege that keeps the chaos, poverty, unemployment, and extreme religious interpretations going and supports corrupt leadership. Others are heirs to class privilege and spend their inheritance fighting both the inequalities and the leadership. Still others are heirs to religious leadership that seeks to bring Muslims back to "right" Islamic practice, and rid the "back-home" countries of corrupt leadership and its supporters. In many Muslim countries, the illiterate majority populations are joining whoever invites their participation to make their lives better. What happens in the United States is a miniversion of the "back-home" struggles. The current "war on terrorism" ignores the fact that much of the violence in the world lies in attempts to dismantle the world as scripted by the West.

Just as Americans fought the American Revolution, other countries do not want a compromised sovereignty nor do they want their countries run by the West. As the current Bush government has begun what many Muslims see as a particularly sinister policy of using Muslim religiosity as an index of potentiality for acts of terrorism, the struggles of Muslims have increased exponentially. For the first time in American history, believers in a faith are experiencing government interference with the practice of that faith. One immigrant male recently related to a reporter for *The Record* (Bergen County, New Jersey) the fact that the FBI probe of immigrant Muslims includes questions about religious practice.[19]

Current immigrant Muslim leadership in America is overwhelmingly male and Salafi. They are also conservative and biased as is the religious leadership in the Muslim world. Even in discussion about Muslim women, male American immigrants control the conversations, speaking for women just as they do in the Muslim world. Arriving in America has not changed some aspects of authority. Immigrant Muslim leadership is persistent in traditions that suppress women's voices by keeping them focused on their material well-being and marriage. So, in addition to wonderful cultural artifacts, they have brought misogyny and Muslim-world patriarchy along with them. After missteps and/or outright blunders in the public space on issues of gender, politics, domestic policy, and race transnational Muslims continue to cling to cultural, not Islamic values.[20] In many ways this focus is a direct outcome of why transnational Muslims came to the United States. They did not come to America to participate in its society; they came to increase their personal material well-being and professional opportunities, hoping to increase the potential for survival of their families here and "back-home" just as many other immigrants have done and continue to do.[21]

Their qualifications for leadership in a society where they have segregated themselves using their own cultural biases for guidance are, therefore, severely compromised. Europe and America are different in societal organization from many of the other places on the globe that transnationals have penetrated.

Who Is Muslim and Who Is Speaking?

In the United States anyone who declares that they are Muslim, just as in Islamic law, is Muslim. The Ahmadiyyah, Shiʿa, Nation of Islam, and Sufi are equally Muslim with those who claim to be Sunni. Even though Sunni Muslims have written books on why these other communities are not Muslim, there is little influential effect in the larger American society. Non-Muslims seeking knowledge about Islam and/or how to become Muslim tend not to be aware of the schisms nor the history and will consider as Muslims whoever claims to be Muslim. Of equal importance, the government and media also tend not to know who is who and readily accept the determinations of orientalists and antagonists.

The question of who speaks for Muslims is of grave concern in America for the community and for non-Muslims. Immigrants have criteria—those who are *madrassah* trained with subsequent qualifications from well-known al-Azhar or from either the universities in Deoband or Aligarh. Next, their families should be known scholars and their articulations of the classical texts should be known. Finally, they must be Arabic speakers. These criteria always have escalating tendencies, if not purposes, created by community scholars. Most of these scholars have had little respect for or influence in their own countries. They tend to believe that, owing to their education and cultural origins, they are morally and intellectually superior to people in the West. That view has structured their cultural isolation in the United States.

The Ahmadis, Ismaili, the Sufis, and the Shi'a, and the indigenous American Muslims are generally seen by the Arab and South Asian center as outcasts. Despite the fact that many of the outcasts possess the prerequisite training, a family lineage of scholars, and may even be Arabic speakers, the view held about these communities from the Muslim world prevents even their consideration in leadership positions. But non-Muslim Americans choose their own conversation partners, preferring those who can hold a conversation. Western scholars used the weakness and arrogance of Arab and South Asian communities against them.

After September 11, 2001, the media combed each Muslim community for spokespersons. Many came forth. Since there was no organization of leaders, any Muslim who could sound authoritative was interviewed on television. Sadly, these instances heralded an immediate need to begin to either groom or consolidate leadership among immigrant Muslims. Is Islam in America to be the Islam in the Muslim world—full of corrupt leadership, patriarchal, bound by a particular interpretation of the Qur'an, only concerned with inner-domestic problems, and oblivious to the needs of others in the larger American society? Or is Islam in America going to assert itself as an American tradition, fully concerned?

There is evidence that the answer to the latter question is, yes. Islam in America will be forged by Muslims into an American tradition. Those cultural traditions that are incompatible with Islamic ideals of justice, care for the poor, participation in society, gender egalitarianism, pluralism, and so forth, will recede from prominence, if not disappear altogether. This is not to say that all of the dissonance currently in the community will also disappear. Some Muslims, like some Christians, Jews, atheists, and others, will remain prejudiced against the others whether that prejudice is based on differences in class, race, ethnicity, or even profession. But generally, the main body of Muslims knows that change or at least an attempt at change is necessary for survival in the United States as well as in the Muslim world. Adoption without loss of identity is possible as the diasporic history of other groups evidences. In the case of immigrant Muslims, too, the settling in will take perhaps a little longer period of time and be a little more painful.

Even as many in government, among the political speakers, and in the media have mounted a considerable campaign to rid the United States of Muslims and to defame Islam as a religion, Muslims and Islam seem here to stay. Each ethnic Muslim community has a stake in being American, and it is by being American that their best contributions to U.S. society are yet to come.

Notes

Chapter 1. Introduction to Immigrant American Muslims

1. Sowell, *Migrations and Cultures*, 371.

2. Wheeler, preface to *Teaching Islam*. [Currently, there are roughly one thousand undergraduate departments and programs in the study of religion in North America. Many of these offer courses on Islam or courses that deal with Islam in a significant manner. Despite the growing interest in and importance of Islam in the undergraduate curricula in religion, there are currently only about one hundred scholars trained in Islamic studies and religious studies in North America. There are many pitfalls, especially in resources. Some of these pitfalls include uneven translations of primary texts, misplaced emphasis on, and ignorance of, other aspects of Islam, dubious comparisons with Judaism and Christianity, and many outright errors and mistakes, which are repeated and perpetuated in introductory texts.

3. If you can find them see Gomez, *Exchanging Our Country Marks;* Austin, *African Muslims in Antebellum America;* and Diouf, *Servants of Allah.*

4. See Winn and Power, *Tea with Terrorists,* and Rosenberg, *The Last Jihad* for fiction regarding Islam and Muslims.

5. See Giroux, "Double Speak."

6. See Project Censored publications dating back to 1994.

7. Ba-Yunus and Kone, "Muslim Americans: A Demographic Report," in *Muslims' Place in the American Public Square,* 314.

8. Jackson, *Islam and the Blackamerican,* 314. Twenty-three in comparison with the numbers given in Ba-Yunus and Kone's *Muslims' Place in the American Public Square,* 314.

9. Lowe, *Immigrant Acts,* 11.

10. Ibid., 6.

11. Van Hear, *New Diasporas,* 4.

12. Safran, "Diasporas in Modern Societies," in *Diaspora: a journal of transnational studies* 1(1): 83–99. See also Schiller, and Appadurai for a more extensive discussion of transnational communities.

13. In migration studies this phase is called the incipient phase. In this phase immigrants have begun to "penetrate," meaning they are just settling in. This phase many take a few decades or a few generations. In the next phase called "new," they have penetrated but not consolidated, while in the last phase, called "classical," they have both penetrated and consolidated. Examples of the last phase are the colonial immigrants of two hundred years ago.

14. Sowell, *Migrations and Cultures,* 7.

Chapter 2. A Nation of Immigrants, Stereotypes, Imaginations

1. Daniels and Graham, *Debating American Immigration,* 7.

2. See Morreale and Carola, *Italian Americans*; Miščevíc and Kwong, *Chinese Americans*; and Muller, *New Strangers in Paradise.*

3. We see in old movies such as *On the Waterfront* and more recent movies such as *The Gangs of New York* how difficult the notion of pluralism can be. The notion of pluralism has historically been antagonistic to claims of anteriority.

4. There are numerous nonfictional accounts written by Irish, Italian, Jewish, and Chinese immigrants of their experiences of American racism and bias.

5. Though the first Europeans were ruthless in both African chattel slavery and Native American genocide, they sought to protect themselves from encroachment by Europe in the Monroe Doctrine in 1823, which was a statement of U.S. policy on the activities and rights of European powers in the Western Hemisphere.

6. Commager, *Documents of American History,* 135.

7. Ibid., 136.

8. Asians are excluded for admission because they are not "white." See discussion of the "free white persons" rule, which goes back to 1790, in Lopez, *White by Law.* In 1924 Congress enacted the National Origins Act which banned the people of East Asia and forbade most immigration from Asian countries. Along with trying to exclude "indigent," and "mentally incompetent" potential citizens, President Coolidge felt that "new arrivals should be limited to our capacity to absorb them into the ranks of good citizenship. Americans must be kept American" (Otis Graham, "The Unfinished Reform: Regulating Immigration in the National Interest," in *Debating American Immigration,* by Daniels and Graham, 127). *American* meant white and Protestant. Readers should not confuse the "white" categories in immigration policies with the "free white persons" rule regarding the internal racial category.

9. According to Ba-Yunus and Kone's article "Muslim Americans," 86 percent of immigrant Muslim Americans are in the professions of engineering/electronics, computer science/data processing, or medicine, 317.

10. Van Hear, *New Diasporas*, 2.

11. Laura Shapiro's review of Weissman, *A Perfect Fit,* in *The New York Review of Books,* July 15, 2001, 16.

12. See discussions on veiling in Jane Smith, *Islam in America.*

13. Bernstein, introduction to *Visions of the East.*

14. Ibid., 3.

15. Hudson and Corrigan, *Religion in America,* 208.

16. Marsden, *Fundamentalism and American Culture,* 3.

17. See Price, "A Fundamentalist Social Gospel," in *Christian Century*, November 28, 1979; Gorrell, *The Age of Social Responsibility;* White and Hopkins, *The Social Gospel.*

18. Bernstein, introduction, in *Visions of the East.*

19. See Alan Nadel's "A Whole New (Disney) World Order: Aladdin, Atomic Power, and the Muslim Middle East," in *Visions of the East*, 185.

20. Goldsmith, "Une seconde jeunesse pour les comptoir colonaux," in *Le Monde Dipolmatique*, Avril 1996, 18–19.

21. Ibid.

22. Hodgson. *Rethinking World History*, 6.

23. See Lutz and Collins, *Reading National Geographic.*

24. Graham-Brown, *Images of Women*, 6.

25. Twain, *The Innocents Abroad.*

26. Armstrong, *Muhammad: A Biography of The Prophet*, 24–26.

27. Said, *Covering Islam*, 5.

28. Quoted in Armstrong, 43.

29. Gaarder, *Sophie's World*, 277.

30. Ibid.

31. Arthur, "Religion, Education and Communication of Values," in *Religion and the Media*, 91.

32. Ibid., 32.

33. Ibid., 34.

34. See http://news.bbc.co.uk/2/hi/programmes/correspondent/3028585.stm.

35. Council on American-Islamic Relations Research Center, *Status of Muslim Civil Rights in the United States.*

36. See http://www.cair-net.org/asp/execsum2004.asp.

Chapter 3. Brief Introduction to Islam

1. See Bukhari, et al., eds., *Muslims' Place in the American Public Square.*

2. See Moore, "Open House: Visibility, Knowledge and Integration. . . ."

3. In keeping with Western modes of inquiry, scholars have categorized the content of the Qur'an like the Bible—chapter and verse. The actual categorizations, *sura* and *ayah* (pl.; *ayat*, sing.), convey a meaning truer in intent to the worldview of the Qur'an.

4. Prophets are given special appellations following their names to both thank Allah for his mercy in sending them and to ask Allah to be merciful toward them in the hereafter. *Pbuh* is an abbreviation for "peace and blessing upon him."

5. All prophets did miraculous things as were expected by their people as proof of their special mission. The prophet Muhammad's miracle was the Qur'an—given to a man who could neither read nor write.

6. Very little is known of the life of Khadijah bint Khuwaylid. This most important woman has gone unreported for fourteen centuries, as has her married life. Mu'awiyah, the fifth caliph of the Muslim community, all but erased Khadyah's contributions to the early Muslim community from history. The Wahhabi in the twentieth century demolished her home.

7. Many writers have incorrectly described the prophet Muhammad (pbuh) as illiterate using modern Western standards, while the qualifications for literacy in the oral tradition of the seventh-century Arabia were quite different. Writing in seventh-century Arabia was an extraordinary skill, the profession of a few.

8. Literally, "the cube." The house dedicated to the One God and built under divine inspiration by the prophet Abraham in what is now Mecca, Saudi Arabia, inside the Great Mosque.

9. Watt, *Muhammad: Prophet and Statesman,* 224.

10. See Murata, *The Tao of Islam,* for more information on this topic.

11. It is important to note here that *Arab* was not a stable category for at least two hundred years after the first revelation was received.

12. Eaton, "The Geographic Expansion of Islam," in *The Spread of Islam,* 72.

13. See Ullmann, *Islamic Medicine,* or Grant, et al., eds., *The Foundations of Modern Science in the Middle Ages.*

14. See Hayes, ed., *The Genius of Arab Civilization.*

15. The Ka'ba is a cube-shaped, one-room structure in Mecca, Saudi Arabia. Muslims believe this most important sanctuary in Islam was built by Abraham and Ishmael.

16. The direction toward Mecca that the Muslim faces for prayer.

17. *Hijra* refers to the emigration of the prophet Muhammad (pbuh) from Mecca to Yathrib (Medina) after years of persecution.

18. Ramadan is the ninth lunar month. It is the month in which Muslims fast, from sunrise to sunset, from secular activities including eating and drinking for thirty days to commemorate the prophet Muhammad's (pbuh) reception of the first portions of the Qur'an.

Chapter 4. South Asian History in Overview

1. See Stein, *History of India.*

2. Ibid., 111.

3. Smith, Wilfred, *Islam in Modern History,* 286. Also see Tamimi, ed., *Power-Sharing Islam?*

4. Sunderland, "The New Movement in India."

5. Indian history has already forgotten that Gandhi's teacher and co-patriot was a Muslim named Abdul Ghaffar Khan. See *Non-Violent Soldier of Islam*, by Eknath Easwaran, 2nd ed. Tomales, Calif.: Nilgiri Press, 1999.

6. Yann, *Shi'ite Islam,* 4.

7. Ibid., 6.

8. Tabatabi, Allamah Sayyid Muhammad Husayn. *Shi'ite Islam.*

9. Sachedina, "A Minority Within a Minority," in *Muslim Communities in North America,* 3.

10. Ibid., 4.

11. Ibid., 7.

12. For more historical information on this community see Blank, *Mullahs on the Mainframe,* and Daftary, *Medieval Isma'ilis History and Thought.*

13. Lewis, *Islamic Britain,* 36.

14. Nielsen, *Religions of the World,* 143–44.

15. Carmody, *Religious Woman,* 43.

16. Ibid., 44.

17. Ibid., 163–64.

18. Interview with Pakistani woman aged forty-eight on February 3, 2000.

19. Carmody, *Religious Woman*, 44.

20. Repeat interview with Alia, Sadia, and Fatima on August 4, 2000. [First interviewed on March 6, 2000.]

Chapter 5. South Asian Culture

1. Interview with Indian woman in June 2000.

2. *The Oprah Winfrey Show*, August 8, 2000.

3. Moore, *Al-Mughtaribun*, 56.

4. Bhabha, *The Location of Culture*, 2.

5. Ungar, *Fresh Blood*, 23.

6. Bouvier, *Peaceful Invasion*, 94.

7. Interview with South Asian female aged fifty-two on February 12, 2000.

8. Interview with South Asian female aged forty-eight on February 12, 2000.

9. The exact number of Muslims in the United States is unknown. Whatever the number of American Muslims, Muslims of South Asian descent comprise about 26.4 percent of them.

10. Interview with South Asian woman aged twenty-nine on March 10, 2000.

11. My students often talk about living between two worlds. At home they speak a mixture of Urdu and English while listening to lectures on the importance of getting A's at any cost as the honor of the family depends on it. At school they are confronted with academic criteria that can severely penalize success at any cost. Some take out their frustrations by deliberately participating in the forbidden such as taking drugs, drinking alcohol, or having premarital sex.

12. Interview with Mirza Khan on January 20, 2000.

13. Group interview at DePaul University, Chicago, in June 2000.

14. Interview with South Asian couple on June 6, 2000.

15. Interview with Sadia Khan on May 15, 2000.

16. Interview with Samir Ali on May 15, 2000.

17. Ibid.

18. Interview with Fatima, Alia, and Sadia on March 6, 2000.

19. Ibid.

20. Interview with Pakistani man aged twenty-five on July 5, 2000.

21. Interview with Indian man aged twenty-four on July 5, 2000.

22. Ibid.

23. Maira, "Identity dub: the paradoxes of an Indian American youth subculture," in *Cultural Anthropology*, vol. 14, no. 1 (February 1999), 29.

24. Ibid., 30.

25. Ibid., 33.

26. Ibid., 34.

27. Interview with South Asian woman aged thirty.

Chapter 6. Islam and the Arabs

1. Daniel, *Islam and The West*, 13.

2. Armstrong, *Muhammad: A Biography of The Prophet*, 24.

3. Hodgson, *Rethinking World History,* 6.

4. Graham-Brown, *Images of Women,* 6.

5. Ibid., 5.

6. Ibid., 6.

7. Lawrence, *Shattering the Myth,* 5.

8. Arthur, "Media Mythologies," in *Religion and the Media,* 27.

9. *Project Censored.*

10. Huntington, *Who Are We?*

11. Ibid., xv.

12. Barakat, *The Arab World,* 12.

Chapter 7. Arab Muslims in the United States

1. Stevens, "Mosque: a Religious, Political Tug of War," in *Chicago Tribune,* July 27, 2000, 1.

2. Ibid., 25.

3. Lovell, "Islam in the United States: Past and Present," in *The Muslim Community in North America,* 94.

4. Lebor, *A Heart Turned East,* 250.

5. See Lynd et al., eds., *Homeland: Oral Histories of Palestine and Palestinians;* Gorkin and Othman, *Three Mothers, Three Daughters;* and Said, *Out of Place.*

6. Haddad and Lummis, *Islamic Values in the United States,* 11.

7. Stewart and Bennett, *American Cultural Patterns,* x.

8. Ibid., 6.

9. Nydell, *Understanding Arabs,* 21.

10. Stewart and Bennett, *American Cultural Patterns,* 14.

11. Interview with fifteen-year-old Sudanese girl, in early September, 2001.

12. Najjar. *Portraits of Palestinian Women,* 4.

13. Ibid., 9–10.

14. Ibid., 18.

15. Interview with Maryam Ali in September 2001.

16. Ibid.

17. This story is recounted by Harris in *Guarding the Secrets.*

18. Interview with Maryam Ali.

19. Interview with Ilham Ahmed in September 2001.

20. It is important to note that not all Arabs are Muslim, the majority of Arab Americans are Christian; and not all Americans of Egyptian descent are Muslim, some are Coptic Christians.

21. Interview with sixteen-year-old Sudanese-American high school student.

22. Interview with fourteen-year-old Sudanese-American high school student.

Chapter 8. Iranian Muslim Immigrants: The Philosopher Poets

1. One of the most frequent pieces of misinformation is the persistent "Saddam Hussein kills his own people." Sunni Muslims are a minority population in Iraq along with Kurds who are not Arabs. Hussein clearly does not see these people as "his own."

2. Nasr, "Introduction" to *Shi'ism: Doctrines, Thought and Spirituality,* 1.

3. See http://www.haruth.com/JewsIran.html and http://www.persianoutpost.com/htdocs/iranianjews.html.

4. Interview with Dr. Ahmad Bastani, July 30, 2000.

5. See http://jamaats.mumineen.org/sf/ghadir.html.

6. Ibid.

7. Yann, Richard. *Shi'ite Islam,* 1995.

8. Momen, *An Introduction to Shi'i Islam,* 63.

9. Yann, 44.

10. "Cults are all of those religious groups which are publicly regarded as being too far removed from the religious mainstream to qualify as members of the legitimate American religious genus, but are instead seen as mutants who constitute a new breed." Glock and Stark, *Christian Beliefs and Anti-Semitism,* 84. This is certainly not true of Shi'a Muslims.

11. Macleod, "Can Iran Be Forgiven?," in *Time Magazine,* 152, no. 5 (August 1998): 44.

12. Interview with Jafar on June 12, 2000.

13. Modarresi, "Iranian Americans, Residents, Immigrants, Citizens," in *Goftegoo Magazine: Culture and Social* (Spring 2000), no. 27, 127.

14. Afkhami, *Women in Exile,* 1.

15. Naficy, *The Making of Exile Cultures,* xiii.

16. Afkhami, 6.

17. Interview with Ali Mirkhani on September 27, 2000.

18. See Afkhami, "Prologue," in *Women in Exile.*

19. Interview with Ali Mirkhani.

20. Ibid.

21. See Yalgani, *Two Sisters: Stories,* and Naficy, *Muddy Shoes* as introductions to Iranian-American literature.

22. See text at http://userwww.service.emory.edu/~sevrahi/PN/Texts/NTtimes.html.

23. Rajavi, Maryam. *Islam and Women's Equality.*

24. Mirkhani interview.

25. Ibid.

26. Ghanea Bassiri, *Competing Visions of Islam in the United States,* 44.

27. Bagheri, B. "A Wedding, Tehrani Style," 2. http://www.persianoutpost.com/htdocs/perswed.html.

28. See http://www.persianoutpost.com. Also this ceremony was talked about in an interview with Shireen Mogadam on January 8, 2000.

29. Benard and Khalilzad, *The Government of God,* 97.

30. Dallalfar, "The Iranian Ethnic Economy in Los Angeles," in *Family and Gender Among American Muslims,* 107–128.

31. Mir-Hosseini, *Islam and Gender,* ix.

Chapter 9. Living on the Margins: Chinese and Somali American Muslims

1. Interview with Amy Lee, October 2000.

2. Dillon, *China's Muslims,* 1.

3. Gladney, *Muslim Chinese,* 37.

4. Ibid., 12.

5. Li and Luckert, *Mythology and Folklore of the Hui*, 19.

6. Much of this information was gleaned from a conversation with Angelica Cedzich, who is a professor of Chinese Religions at DePaul University in Chicago.

7. Jaschok and Jingjun, *The History of Women's Mosques in Chinese Islam,* 45.

8. Ibid., 55.

9. Ibid., 4.

10. Ibid., 83.

11. Ibid., 153.

12. Gladney, *Muslim Chinese,* xiv.

13. Ibid., 2

14. See Miščevíc and Kwong, *Chinese Americans.*

15. Sung, "Chinese Immigration to the United States" in *Contemporary American Immigration,* 11.

16. See Miščevíc and Kwong, *Chinese Americans*, 53–65.

17. Ibid., 83–105.

18. At DePaul University in the spring of 2000, a ten-week program, "Exploring Muslim Cultures," had a seminar led by Professor Dru Gladney. Chicago's Chinese American Muslims attended and expressed tearful gratitude at this small acknowledgment of their existence. Notably, South Asian and Arab Muslims were absent.

19. Liebenberg, "Chinese Muslims in Los Angeles Share Bitter History, Religious Devotion," in *Pacific News Services*, February 22, 2002.

20. Helander, "Somalia," in *Islam Outside the Arab World,* 41.

21. Ibid., 48.

22. Phelps, Depass, and Powell, "Minnesota Somalis send millions back to East Africa."

23. Interview with twenty-three-year-old female Somali college student on November 12, 2001.

24. Williams, "Somalis in Minnesota."

Chapter 10. Global Islam in America: The Mix and the Challenges

1. Deweese, *Islamization and Native Religion in the Golden Horde*, 24.

2. See Deweese for more information.

3. Descendants of the Prophet (pbuh) include Muslims in Morocco and India.

4. See Abou El Fadl, *Rebellion and Violence in Islamic Law.* His chapter, "Rebellion, insurgency, and brigandage," focuses on this issue especially, 239–40.

5. Ibid., 14.

6. Ibid., 15–16.

7. Of course China's history and its somewhat closed society for a number of decades have also contributed to the silence surrounding Chinese Islam.

8. Abu El Fadl, *And God Knows the Soldiers*, 24–25.

9. See Qutb, *In the Shade of The Qur'an.*

10. See A' la Maududi, *Purdah and the Status of Women in Islam.* This text was a staple of American Islamic bookstores in the 1970s and 1980s. It is dehumanizing to women and was marketed as one of the most authentic treatments of women in Islam.

11. Scholarship regarding immigrants and especially Muslim immigrants has always focused on a "brain drain." This is in actuality not really accurate because the transnationals are always enriching the knowledge-base and the quality of life in the root society.

12. Mamdani, *When Victims Become Killers,* 23.

13. I suspect that this issue is discussed at length in researches on transnational corporations; Samuel Huntington certainly addresses it in his recent text.

14. See "The War on Terror/Why the Hate," *Time,* Oct. 1, 2002; "A Kinder, Gentler Koran," *Time,* Aug. 19, 2002; "Struggle for the Soul of Islam," *Time,* Sept. 13, 2004.

15. This scenario is interesting since Judaism has been unwelcome in the United States until very recently, and some Christians still have difficulty tolerating Jews.

16. African American Muslim prisoners began the litigations for changing their names to Muslim names, pork-free diets, the right to pray five times daily, and to pray as a congregation on Fridays in the 1950s. Other African American Muslims had for decades put an Islamic presence on the streets of major cities by their dress, behavior, community centers, and *masajid.*

17. See Mamdani, *When Victims Become Killers,* 13.

18. Ibid.

19. "Legal Aid Offered to those Queried in War on Terror." *The Record* (Bergen County, New Jersey), August 12, 2004, A15.

20. One clear example of this point is when an African American attorney with the American Muslim Council requested that the organization keep its books up-to-date and hire an accountant. This request was made simultaneous with the attorney's assertion that some black Americans had had much different encounters with the Jewish communities here than Arabs and Jews in Israel. Needless to say, he was forced to leave the organization.

21. Members of both the Irish and Jewish communities, to name just two, support and are expected to continue to support causes in other nation states.

Bibliography

Abdul A'la Maududi, Syed. *Purdah and the Status of Women in Islam*. Lahore, Pakistan: Islamic Publications Limited, 1972.

Abou El Fadl, Khaled. *And God Knows the Soldiers*. New York: University Press of America, 2001.

———. *Rebellion and Violence in Islamic Law*. New York: Cambridge University Press, 2001.

Afkhami, Mahnaz, ed. *Women in Exile*. Charlottesville: University Press of Virginia, 1994.

Appadurai, Arjun. *Modernity at Large: Cultural Dimensions of Globalism*. Minneapolis: University of Minnesota Press, 1996.

Armstrong, Karen. *Muhammad: A Biography of The Prophet*. New York: HarperCollins, 1992.

Arthur, Chris. "Religion, Education and Communication of Values." In *Religion and the Media*, edited by Chris Arthur. Cardiff: University of Wales Press, 1993.

———. "Media Mythologies." In *Religion and the Media*, edited by Chris Arthur. Cardiff: University of Wales Press, 1993.

Austin, Allan D. *African Muslims in Antebellum America*. New York, Routledge, 1997.

Ba-Yunus, Ilyas, and Kassim Kone, "Muslim Americans: A Demographic Report." In *Muslims' Place in the American Public Square*, edited by Zahid H. Bukhari, Sulayman S. Nyang, Mumtaz Ahmad, and John L. Esposito. Lanham, Md.: AltaMira Press, 2004.

Barakat, Halim. *The Arab World: Society, Culture, and State*. Los Angeles: University of California Press, 1993.

Benard, Cheryl, and Zalmay Khalilzad. *The Government of God: Iran's Islamic Republic*. New York: Columbia University Press, 1984.

Bernstein, Matthew. "Introduction." In *Visions of the East*, edited by Matthew Bernstein and Gaylyn Studlar. New Brunswick: Rutgers University Press, 1997.

Bhabha, Homi. *The Location of Culture*. New York: Routledge, 2004.

Blank, Jonah. *Mullahs on the Mainframe*. Chicago: University of Chicago Press, 2001.

Bouvier, Leon F. *Peaceful Invasion: Immigration and Changing America*. Lanham, Md.: University Press of America, 1992.

Bukhari, Zahid H., Sulayman S. Nyang, Mumtaz Amad, and John L. Esposito, eds. *Muslims' Place in the American Public Square*. Lanham, Md.: AltaMira Press, 2004.

Carmody, Denise Larder. *Religious Woman*. New York: Crossroad Publishing, 1991.

Commager, Henry Steele. *Documents of American History*. 10th ed. Englewood Cliffs, N.J.: Prentice-Hall, 1988.

Council on American-Islamic Relations Research Center. *The Status of Muslim Civil Rights in the United States: Unveiling Prejudice*. Washington, D.C., 1997.

Daftary, Farhad. *Medieval Isma'ili History and Thought*. Cambridge, U.K.: University of Cambridge Press, 1996.

Dallalfar, Arlene. "The Iranian Ethnic Economy in Los Angeles." In *Family and Gender Among American Muslims*, edited by Barbara Aswad and Barbara Bilge. Philadelphia: Temple University Press, 1996.

Daniel, Norman. *Islam and the West*. Chatham, N.Y.: Oneworld Publications, 1993.

Daniels, Roger, and Otis L. Graham. *Debating American Immigration: 1882–Present*. New York: Rowman and Littlefield, 2001.

Danquah, Meri Nana-Ama. *Becoming American: Personal Essays by First Generation Immigrant Women*. New York: Hyperion, 2001.

Deweese, Devin. *Islamization and Native Religion in the Golden Horde*. University Park: Pennsylvania State University Press, 1994.

Dillon, Michael. *China's Muslims*. New York: Oxford University Press, 1996.

Diouf, Sylvaine. *Servants of Allah*. New York: New York University Press, 1998.

Eaton, Richard M. "The Geographic Expansion of Islam." In *The Spread of Islam*, edited by Clarice Swisher. San Diego, Calif.: Greenhaven Press, 1998.

Gaarder, Jostein. *Sophie's World: A Novel About the History of Philosophy*. Translated by Paulette Moller. New York: Berkley Books, 1996.

Ghanea Bassiri, Kambiz. *Competing Visions of Islam in the United States: A Study of Los Angeles*. Westport, Conn.: Greenwood Press, 1997.

Giroux, Henry. *"Double Speak and the Politics of Dissent,"* at http://dissidentvoice.org/Aug04/Giroux0820.htm.

Gladney, Dru. *Muslim Chinese*. Cambridge: Council on East Asian Studies, Harvard University, 1996.

Glock, Charles Y., and Rodney Stark. *Christian Beliefs and Anti-Semitism*. New York: Harper and Row, 1966.

Goldsmith, Edward. *"Une seconde jeunesse pour les comptoir colonaux."* In *Le Monde Dipolmatique*, Avril 1996, 18–19.

Gomez, Michael A. *Exchanging Our Country Marks*. Chapel Hill: The University of North Carolina Press, 1998.

Gorkin, Michael, and Rafiqa Othman. *Three Mothers, Three Daughters: Palestinian Women's Stories*. Berkeley: University of California Press, 1996.

Gorrell, Donal K. *The Age of Social Responsibility: The Social Gospel in the Progressive Era, 1900–1920*. Macon, Ga.: Mercer University Press, 1988.

Graham-Brown, Sarah. *Images of Women: The Portrayal of Women in Photography of the Middle East 1860–1950*. London: Quartet Books, 1988.

Grant, Edward, George Basalla, and Owen Hannaway, eds. *The Foundations of Modern Science in the Middle Ages: Their Religious, Institutional and Intellectual Contexts*. Cambridge, Mass.: Cambridge University Press, 1996.

Haddad, Yvonne Y., and Adair T. Lummis. *Islamic Values in the United States*. New York: Oxford University Press, 1987.

Harris, Ellen. *Guarding the Secrets: Palestinian Terrorism and a Father's Murder of His Too-American Daughter*. New York: Scribner, 1995.

Hayes, J. R., ed. *The Genius of Arab Civilization*. 2nd ed. Cambridge: MIT Press, 1983.

Helander, Bernhard. "Somalia." In *Islam Outside the Arab World*. Edited by David Westerland and Ingvar Svanberg. Surrey, U.K.: Curzon Press, 1999.

Hodgson, Marshall G. S. *Rethinking World History*. New York: Cambridge University Press, 1993.

Hudson, Winthrop, and John Corrigan. *Religion in America*. 5th ed. New York: Macmillan, 1992.

Huntington, Samuel. *Who Are We?: The Challenges to America's National Identity*. New York: Simon and Schuster, 2004.

Jackson, Sherman A. *Islam and the Blackamerican*. New York: Oxford University Press, 2005.

Jaschok, Maria, and Shui Jingjun. *The History of Women's Mosques in Chinese Islam: A Mosque of Their Own*. Surry, U.K.: Curzon Press, 2000.

Lawrence, Bruce. *Shattering the Myth: Islam Beyond Violence*. Princeton: University of Princeton Press, 1998.

Lebor, Adam. *A Heart Turned East*. New York: St. Martin's Press, 1997.

Lewis, Philip. *Islamic Britain*. New York: I. B. Tauris, 1994.

Li, Shujiang, and Karl W. Luckert. *Mythology and Folklore of the Hui, A Muslim Chinese People*. Albany: State University of New York Press, 1994.

Liebenberg, Anna Sophie. "Chinese Muslims in Los Angeles Share Bitter History, Religious Devotion." *Pacific News Service*, February 22, 2002.

Lopez, Haney. *White by Law*. New York: New York University Press, 1996.

Lovell, Emily Kalled. "Islam in the United States: Past and Present." In *The Muslim Community in North America*, edited by Earle Waugh, Baha Abu-Laban, and Regula Qureshi. Edmonton: University of Alberta Press, 1983.

Lowe, Lisa. *Immigrant Acts: On Asian American Cultural Politics*. Durham, N.C.: Duke University Press, 1996.

Lutz, Catherine A., and Jane L. Collins. *Reading National Geographic*. Chicago: University of Chicago Press, 1993.

Lynd, Staughton, Same Bahour, and Alice Lynd. *Homeland: Oral Histories of Palestine and Palestinians*. Northhampton, Mass.: Interlink, 1998.

Macleod, Scott. "Can Iran Be Forgiven?," *Time* 152, no. 5 (August 1998).

Maira, Sunaina. "Identity dub: the paradoxes of an Indian American youth subculture: New York mix." In *Cultural Anthropology*, vol. 14, no. 1 (February 1999).

Mamdani, Mahmood. *When Victims Become Killers*. Princeton: Princeton University Press, 2001.

Marsden, George. *Fundamentalism and American Culture*. New York: Oxford University Press, 1980.

McGown, Rima Berns. *Muslims in the Diaspora: The Somali Communities of London and Toronto*. Toronto: University of Toronto Press, 1999.

Mir-Hosseini, Ziba. *Islam and Gender*. Princeton: Princeton University Press, 1999.

Miščevíc, Dusanka, and Peter Kwong. *Chinese Americans: The Immigrant Experience*. Reno, Nev.: Hugh Lauter Levin Associates, 2000.

Modarresi, Ali. "Iranian Americans, Residents, Immigrants, Citizens." In *Goftegoo Magazine: Culture and Social,* no. 27 (Spring 2000).

Momen, Moojan. *An Introduction to Shi'i Islam.* New Haven: Yale University Press, 1985.

Moore, Kathleen. "Open House: Visibility, Knowledge and Integration of Muslims in the United States." In *Muslims in the United States,* edited by Philippa Strum and Danielle Tarantolo. Washington, D.C.: Woodrow Wilson International Center for Scholars, 2003.

———. *Al-Mughtaribun: American Law and the Transformation of Muslim Life in the United States.* Albany: State University of New York Press, 1995.

Morreale, Ben, and Robert Carola. *Italian Americans: The Immigrant Experience.* Reno, Nev.: Hugh Lauter Levin Associates, 2000.

Muller, Gilbert H. *New Strangers in Paradise: The Immigrant Experience and Contemporary American Fiction.* Lexington: University Press of Kentucky, 1999.

Murata, Sachiko. *The Tao of Islam.* Albany: State University of New York Press, 1992.

Nadel, Alan. "A Whole New (Disney) World Order: Aladdin, Atomic Power, and the Muslim Middle East," in *Visions of the East* by Matthew Bernstein and Gaylyn Studlar. New Brunswick: Rutgers University Press, 1997.

Naficy, Hamid. *The Making of Exile Cultures.* Minneapolis: University of Minnesota Press, 1993.

———. *Muddy Shoes.* Los Angeles: Beyond Baroque Foundation, 1999.

Najjar, Orayb Aref. *Portraits of Palestinian Women.* Salt Lake City: University of Utah Press, 1992.

Nasr, Seyyed Hossein. "Introduction." In *Shi'ism: Doctrines, Thought and Spirituality,* edited by Seyyed Hossein Nasr, Hamid Dabasi, and Seyyed Vali Reza Nasr. Albany: State University of New York Press, 1988.

Nielsen, Niels C., Jr. *Religions of the World.* New York: St. Martin's Press, 1983.

Nydell, Margaret K. *Understanding Arabs.* Yarmouth, Maine: Intercultural Press, 1999.

Phelps, David, Dee DePass, and Joy Powell. "Minnesota Somalis Send Millions Back to East Africa." In *Minnesota Star Tribune,* November 19, 2000.

Price, Richard M. "A Fundametalist Social Gospel." In *Christian Century,* November 28, 1979.

Project Censored. http://www.projectcensored.org/publications.

Qutb, Sayyid. *In the Shade of the Qur'an.* London: MWH London Publishers, 1979.

Rajavi, Maryam. *Islam and Women's Equality.* Auvers-sur-Oise, France: The National Council of Resistance of Iran, 1995.

Rosenberg, Joel. *The Last Jihad.* New York: Forge Books, 2003.

Sachedina, Abdulaziz. "A Minority Within a Minority: The Case of the Shi'a in North America." In *Muslim Communities in North America,* edited by Yvonne Haddad and Jane I. Smith. Albany: State University of New York Press, 1994.

Safran, William. "Diasporas in Modern Societies: Myths of Homeland and Return." In *Disapora: a journal of transnational studies,* 1(1): 83–99.

Said, Edward. *Covering Islam*. New York: Vintage Press, 1997.

———. *Out of Place: A Memoir*. New York: Knopf, 1999.

Schiller, Nina Glick. *Georges Woke Up Laughing: Long-Distance Nationalism and the Search for Home*. Durham, N.C.: Duke University Press, 2001.

Smith, Jane I. *Islam in America*. New York: Columbia University Press, 1999.

Smith, Wilfred Cantwell. *Islam in Modern History*. Princeton: Princeton University Press, 1977.

Sowell, Thomas. *Migrations and Cultures: A Worldview*. New York: Basic Books, 1996.

Stein, Burton. *History of India*. Malden, Mass.: Blackwell Publishers, 1998.

Stevens, Darlene Gavron. "Mosque: A Religious, Political Tug of War," In *Chicago Tribune*, July 27, 2000, 1.

Stewart, Edward C., and Milton J. Bennett. *American Cultural Patterns*. Yarmouth, Maine: Intercultural Press, 1991.

Strum, Philippa, and Danielle Tarantolo, eds. *Muslims in the United States*. Washington, D.C.: Woodrow Wilson International Center for Scholars, 2003.

Sunderland, Jabez T. "The New Movement in India." In *Atlantic Monthly*, issue 102 (October 1908), 526–535.

Sung, Betty Lee. "Chinese Immigration to the United States." In *Contemporary American Immigration: Non-European*, edited by Dennis Lawrence Cuddy. Boston: Twayne, 1998.

Tabatabi, Allamah Sayyid Muhammad. *Shi'ite Islam*. Houston: Free Islamic Literature, 1971.

Tamimi, Azzam, ed. *Power-Sharing Islam?* London: Liberty for Muslim World Publications, 1993.

Twain, Mark. *The Innocents Abroad. Roughing It*. Edited by Guy Cardwell. New York: Library of America, 1984.

Ullman, M. *Islamic Medicine*. Edinburgh: Edinburgh University Press, 1978.

Ungar, Sanford J. *Fresh Blood: The New American Immigrants*. Chicago: University of Illinois Press, 1998.

Van Hear, Nicholas. *New Diasporas: The mass exodus, dispersal and regrouping of migrant communities*. Seattle: University of Washington Press, 1998.

Watt, Montgomery W. *Muhammad: Prophet and Statesman*. New York: Oxford University Press, 1961.

Weissman, Jenna. *A Perfect Fit*. New York: Henry Holt, 2001.

Wheeler, Brannon M., ed. *Teaching Islam*. New York, Oxford University Press, 2003.

White, Ronald C., Jr., and C. Howard Hopkins. *The Social Gospel: Religion and Reform in Changing America*. Philadelphia: Temple University Press, 1976.

Williams, Brandt. "Somalis in Minnesota." Minnesota Public Radio. http://news.minnesota.publicradio.org/features/200202/04_williamsb_africans/somalis.htm.

Winn, Craig, and Ken Power. *Tea with Terrorists*. Charlottesville, Va.: CricketSong Books, 2002.

Yann, Richard. *Shi'ite Islam*. Oxford, U.K.: Blackwell Publishers, 1995.

Index

Aminah Beverly McCloud is professor of Islamic Studies at DePaul University and director of the Islamic World Studies Program. She is also editor of *The Journal of Islamic Law and Culture*. She is the author of *African American Islam* (1995) and *Questions of Faith* (1999), as well as the author of many articles and chapters in texts.